Russell Chamberlin is a professional writer, the author of more than twenty books on social history. Until recently, the majority of these were concerned with the Italian Renaissance, but it was in tracing the effects of the Renaissance on English history that he became more and more involved in English urban history. 'I became intrigued with the shape of our town hall. Why, I wondered, did an honest Jacobean building made of local oak try to pretend to be an Italian building made of marble?'

He lives in Guildford, an 'English country town' which, though within the gravitational pull of London, stubbornly maintains its own identity.

Charlie Waite was an actor for ten years before taking up professional photography in 1974. He was commissioned to do the photography for the *National Trust Book of Long Walks* and the sequel *Long Walks in France*, and has undertaken various other commissions for the National Trust. He is married to an actress, has one daughter and lives in London.

RUSSELL CHAMBERLIN

The National Trust Book of the English Country Town

with photographs by Charlie Waite

GRAFTON BOOKS

A Division of the Collins Publishing Group

LONDON GLASGOW
TORONTO SYDNEY AUCKLAND

Grafton Books
A Division of the Collins Publishing Group
8 Grafton Street, London W1X 3LA

Published by Grafton Books 1986

First published in Great Britain by
Webb & Bower (Publishers) Limited
in collaboration with the National Trust 1983
under the title *The English Country Town*

ISBN 0-586-06392-7

Printed and bound in Great Britain by
Collins, Glasgow

Set in Ehrhardt

Contents

Now thus much without vanity may it be aserted that if all persons, both Ladies, much more gentlemen, would spend some of their tyme in Journeys to visit their native Land, and be curious to inform themselves and make observations of the pleasant prospects, good buildings different produces and manufactures of each place ... it would form such an Idea of England, add much to its Glory and Esteem in our minds and cure the evil itch of over-valueing foreign parts.

CELIA FIENNES: *The Journeys*

Selected English Country Towns

AVON
Bath

BEDFORDSHIRE
Bedford

BERKSHIRE
Hungerford

BUCKINGHAMSHIRE
Aylesbury
High Wycombe

CAMBRIDGESHIRE
Cambridge
Ely
Wisbech

CHESHIRE
Chester

CORNWALL
Bodmin
Padstow

CUMBRIA
Alston

DERBYSHIRE
Bakewell
Wirksworth

DEVON
Barnstaple
Exeter
Totnes

DORSET
Dorchester
Lyme Regis
Shaftesbury
Wareham

DURHAM
Barnard Castle
Durham
Escomb

EAST SUSSEX
Rye
Winchelsea

ESSEX
Colchester

GLOUCESTERSHIRE
Cheltenham
Chipping Campden
Cirencester
Tewkesbury

GREATER LONDON
Chiswick
Richmond

HAMPSHIRE
Alresford
Winchester

HEREFORD & WORCESTER
Bewdley
Droitwich
Hereford
Worcester

HERTFORDSHIRE
Berkhamsted
St Albans

KENT
Canterbury
Maidstone
Rochester

LANCASHIRE
Accrington
Barrow-in-Furness
Lancaster
Ormskirk

LINCOLNSHIRE
Gainsborough
Grantham
Lincoln
Stamford

NORFOLK
Caister-by-Norwich
Castle Acre
Cromer
King's Lynn
Norwich
Thetford
Wymondham

NORTHAMPTONSHIRE
Oundle

NORTHUMBERLAND
Alnwick
Berwick-upon-Tweed
Hexham
Housesteads
Warkworth

NORTH YORKSHIRE
Richmond
Ripon
Skipton
York

OXFORDSHIRE
Oxford
Thame
Wantage

SHROPSHIRE
Ludlow
Shrewsbury
Wroxeter

SOMERSET
Glastonbury
Wells

SUFFOLK
Bury St Edmunds
Dunwich
Ipswich
Lavenham

SURREY
Cranleigh
Dorking
Eashing
Epsom
Farnham
Godalming
Guildford

TYNE AND WEAR
Newcastle

WARWICKSHIRE
Stratford-upon-Avon

WEST MIDLANDS
Birmingham
Coventry

WEST SUSSEX
Arundel
Chichester
Petworth

WEST YORKSHIRE
Haworth
Wakefield

WILTSHIRE
Bradford-upon-Avon
Malmesbury
Salisbury
Swindon

The English Counties

NORTHUMBERLAND

TYNE AND WEAR

DURHAM

CLEVELAND

CUMBRIA

NORTH YORKSHIRE

LANCASHIRE

WEST YORKSHIRE

HUMBERSIDE

GREATER MANCHESTER

MERSEYSIDE

SOUTH YORKSHIRE

CHESHIRE

DERBYSHIRE

LINCOLNSHIRE

NOTTINGHAMSHIRE

STAFFORDSHIRE

SHROPSHIRE

LEICESTERSHIRE

NORFOLK

WEST MIDLANDS

CAMBRIDGESHIRE

NORTHAMPTON-SHIRE

WARWICK-SHIRE

SUFFOLK

HEREFORD AND WORCESTER

BEDFORDSHIRE

BUCKINGHAM-SHIRE

HERTFORD-SHIRE

ESSEX

GLOUCESTERSHIRE

OXFORDSHIRE

GREATER LONDON

AVON

BERKSHIRE

WILTSHIRE

SURREY

KENT

SOMERSET

HAMPSHIRE

WEST SUSSEX

EAST SUSSEX

DEVON

DORSET

ISLE OF WIGHT

CORNWALL

Introduction
Traveller's View

The ideal way to enter a town on the first occasion is by train. If the railway track no longer exists, but has been sacrificed to the chimera of automotive transport, then the traveller who wants to experience the town as an organic whole, and not simply as a chance collection of structures, should come in by river. If neither rail nor river transport exists then the only other choice is the top deck of a double-decker bus whence it is possible to see at least the outlines of the fields that lie beneath and behind the fringe of suburbia.

For the twentieth century's major contribution to the creation of urban communities has been the construction of suburbs, fringing the centre with a mildew of small houses, filling stations, carpet warehouses, derelict lots and used-car showrooms. In some of our smaller towns and cities subsoil unsuitable for building, or the presence of a powerful, long-established landowner, has preserved an area of green just outside the town, permitting the illusion that the town retains still its ancient shape. Thus at Alnwick in Northumbria the vast castle of the Dukes of Northumberland puts a dramatic term to the northern edge of the town. The traveller approaching the town from the Berwick road sees Alnwick first as a tremendous range of castellated walls and towers rising up sheer from the water-meadows. The road winds up the steep hill under the very shadow of the castle, taking the traveller instantly into the heart of the town. At Ludlow in Shropshire a similar effect is produced from entirely different causes. The common land known as Whitcliff is separated physically from the town first by the barrier of the river, then by precipitous cliffs so that it is possible to look down from the common to the town lying at its feet. At Guildford in Surrey the boggy nature of the water-meadows on the south has inhibited building: it is thus possible to walk along by the river's edge on green fields to within a few yards of the High

Street, the great shoulders of the Downs rising up to enclose the walker as the town is approached from this angle.

But even in these favoured towns, the illusion is limited only to one small area. Elsewhere, as with all other towns, the suburbs mask the shape, flowing formlessly into the surrounding country. Planning laws have halted the ribbon building that raped so much of the English countryside in the 1920s. But in its place has come 'infilling', based on the concept that what is half-ruined might as well be wholly ruined, filling the land between the ribbon-edged roads with a maze of structures. Through all this the road makes its way. Modern traffic routeing, turning streets into one-way conduits that may actually lead away from their goal at certain stages, further confuses the traveller, eliminating finally any sense of arrival. It is only when the buildings begin to thicken, and the No Entry signs to proliferate, that the traveller deduces that he has probably arrived at his goal, the town centre.

But the railway sweeps the traveller through the twentieth-century irrelevances – sometimes adding the bonus of an embankment which gives an unrivalled bird's-eye view of the town. One of the stupendous sights of Europe is the panorama of Durham seen from the high railway viaduct to the east, the vast cathedral and castle rearing up from the gulf beneath, unforgettable in their majesty. And such a view can be obtained only by courtesy of the prodigal labour of Victorian railway engineers. If you approach Norwich from the south during August – just after the wheat has ripened and before it is cut – those same engineers provide the twentieth-century traveller with a view back 2000 years into the past. For there, visible only during this period and from this direction, are the crop-marks outlining the ghost of Roman Caister, all that is left of the town that preceded Norwich.

The railway rarely brings the traveller into the heart of the town: land was too expensive, the value of the new transport system too problematical to allow of such wholesale destruction. Usually the station is half a mile or a mile away, built out in what was open country and connected to the town with a new road christened, as often as not, Victoria Road or Prince of Wales Road or Alma Road if some burst of nineteenth-century patriotism coincided with the building of the road. Otherwise it will be simply Station Road, an unimaginative name perhaps but invaluable as an indicator for the stranger. The vicinity of most stations is today seedy and depressing, the pubs run down, the huge open spaces given over to coal dumps and car parks. But in Chester is a splendid survival – the great Queen Hotel – that gives some indication of the pride and self-confidence of those who built the railways. Born of the railway, the Queen owes much of its present prosperity to the ironic fact that it is the only major hotel with a car park near the town centre. The near life-size statue of Victoria, freshly painted, is hoisted high up on its façade, overlooking the station, the one now almost as much a museum piece as the other.

Unlike the modern trunk roads that circle indecisively around the town centre, Station Road takes the traveller direct to his goal. On the town map, the centre is immediately apparent for here not only are the streets greater in number and shorter in length but they twist and turn and wind irregularly, each curve and corner produced by some factor of local history and not, as in the case of the suburbs, by an abstract decision made on a planning board. The street names, too, tell the same story for each describes a locality – the Buttermarket – or a trade – Weavers' Row. They curve and twist and wind, these central streets and alleys and lanes, debouching into a central space. That space might be a formal square like the great Tuesday Market of King's Lynn, or simply a widening of the road that passes through the town, like the High Street of Marlborough. But it is a major focal point – perhaps the only one if the town is small or if, centuries ago, the lord of the manor was able to grab the lucrative monopoly of market rights.

At eye level and above, the face of the buildings in and around the central square or high street will be clad in their traditional materials – stone or brick or timber. From eye level to ground level the twentieth century makes its characteristic impact in the form of plate glass and standardized plastic fascia. Mostly these have been perpetrated by the great national and international chains which have taken over more and more retail outlets, ousting the small local trader each with his distinctive shop-front and imposing their own strident but monotonous images. Rarely do they contribute anything to the street scene. The branch of Woolworth's in

Ludlow, however, still has its splendid thirties fascia of scarlet and gold – a period piece now, and a disconcerting reminder that this generation's monstrosity may well be the next generation's cherished heritage.

Somewhere near the high street or market-place is the parish church. Its spire or tower might have acted as a beacon to the traveller over many miles but it has a trick of disappearing when only a few yards away. Here, in its refusal to make set pieces of its ceremonial buildings, the English town differs profoundly from its continental counterpart. The older town hall or guildhall and parish church are more likely to be tucked away down an alley-way than dominating a square. Even the cathedral is reticent: in Ripon, it is possible to be within fifty yards of the cathedral and be quite unaware of its existence. In Norwich, the superb church of St Peter Mancroft and the chequered spendour of the guildhall do indeed dominate the central market-place – but this is only since the restructuring of the city centre in the 1930s. Before that, both buildings were tucked away snugly in a maze of streets and buildings. Totnes's guildhall faces the churchyard, forming a little enclave of its own. The English refusal to provide for ceremony gives, as by-product, a marvellously rich texture to the urban fabric: even in quite small towns it is usually necessary to walk every street in the central area before familiarity can be claimed for the whole, instead of taking in two or three ceremonial areas at a glance.

Before World War II our town centres were thickly studded with pubs, most of which would provide accommodation for the traveller, if of a rough and ready sort. But the number of pubs has diminished substantially in response to changing social customs and most of those that remain are reluctant to make the heavy investment of time, space and energy that accommodation demands. Modern hotels tend to be built on the by-pass, with the town in irrelevance on the horizon and, what with one thing and another, the modern traveller is badly served in this matter.

But somewhere in the town centre there will usually be a large, square building with a sober façade and an archway through it leading, usually, to an asphalted car park – but sometimes to an area bright with flowers in tubs. The coaching inn. Its name will perhaps be the George but both the name and the façade are eighteenth-century additions to a far older building, a product of that century's explosion of travel. After signing on in the genuine Georgian reception room and being led across genuinely uneven Tudor floors, the traveller will probably find that his bedroom is, in fact, part of the 'new wing' – a square, blank box furnished in the bland international style and overlooking the car park. But between eighteenth-century façade and twentieth-century box lies a medley of rooms that are part of the town's living history.

And having secured accommodation, the traveller's first need is orientation. The superb British public library system ensures that, somewhere in even the smallest town, there will be a room – or at least a shelf of books – devoted to 'local history'. But that is for more leisurely study, providing the answer to 'Why?' after the traveller has discovered 'What?' Swift orientation is needed during the first few hours in a strange town, and the best place to find this is a local newsagent.

The newsagent/confectioner/tobacconist (and frequently also greengrocer) is the last flowering of the general store which plays such a large part in childhood memories. But that general store with its piles of cheese rubbing shoulders with apples, with its great barrels of rolled oats and brown sugar, with its hams hanging from the ceiling and its floor cluttered with spades and sacks of potatoes and its counter all but invisible under jars of sweets and cardigans in cardboard boxes – that genuine emporium – has been swept into the past along with the chapman and the pedlar, killed off by the specialist shop and the supermarket and, particularly, by the centralized packaging of goods.

But the newsagent continues. The tiny royalty he (and his wife, for always it is a family business) receives from the national newspapers and magazines provides at least a regular income. To it can be added the sale of imperishables – plastic toys, 'fancy' goods, greetings cards. And 'books'. The term 'books', for the country-town newsagent, includes almost anything that can be read but tends to exclude what is normally meant by the word. Thus on display will be a selection of children's garish picture books, the more popular women's magazines, and 'Do-it-yourself' periodicals. But there will be, too, the local newspaper – whose whole purpose is to reflect its community – a guidebook and a handful of picture postcards. The standard of the guidebook can be anything from the excruciatingly dull to the brilliantly presented, and the postcards will, on the whole, be limited to what is 'picturesque'. But newspaper, guidebook and postcards will, between them, serve to give identity to the town.

At 5.30 P.M. sharp the shops close and the town dies. For about half an hour afterwards there is a twitching as the workers in offices and shops and factories make their way home but from 6 P.M. onwards the streets belong to the stranger. There is nothing in England comparable to the amiable continental custom of the promenade when, for a short period in a particular place at a particular time, the townsfolk take the air, maintaining contact with each other at least once in each twenty-four hours. The English eschew this familiarity. This is not to say that social life has ended in the English town: on the contrary, from about 7 P.M. onwards the place is a hive of activity. In the town hall the local amateur operatic company will be rehearsing the Grand March from *Aida*; the classes in art, commercial Spanish, flower arranging, Renaissance history and wood carving will be in full swing in one of the schools. Specialist societies – Theosophists and ufologists, civic amenity, political, spiritual, economic, literary – will all be holding their impassioned debates. Nothing more clearly demonstrates the clubbability of the English than the list of voluntary societies that most local public libraries maintain: those societies seem to cover everything from archery to zoology, each with its Hon Sec and chairman and Annual General Meeting and audited accounts, each with its indication of a lively social life working within the town.

But that is only for the established inhabitants. The traveller passing through has very limited choices. The cinema has been turned into a bingo hall; the theatre promises an amateur performance of *Dear Octopus*; it is too cold to sit in the park; too early to eat. The only certain entertainments are the pub and the town itself.

The pub is one of the few places where the stranger can sit, unmolested, for as long as he likes doing nothing but observing. And there can be no better place to enter the heart of the town, for the people in the pub are the raw material of which the town is made. It was their ancestors, with their quirks and prejudices and strokes of genius and parsimony, who made the town. And it is they who, adapting what they have inherited, adding unconsciously their own prejudices and strokes of genius and parsimony and quirks, are shaping it endlessly for the future. Only when the traveller has heard their accents, listened to their complaints and comments, is he really in a position to understand the shaping of their town, and to begin his own exploration of the physical complex back over perhaps millennia.

This book is an attempt to tell the story of the growth of our towns in terms of their topography, and of their surviving historic buildings and institutions.

There is, of course, no adequate definition of the word 'town' and very considerable uncertainty as to what distinguishes a 'town' from a 'city' or a 'village'. Size is no help. In Surrey, the village of Cranleigh has a population of over 11,000 whereas Richmond in Yorkshire has a population of less than 700 – but is indubitably a town. At the other end of the scale, Chichester (population 25,000) is a city whereas Guildford (population 60,000) is not. And to compound ambiguities, the pernicious Local Government Act of 1974, in lumping distinct communities together for the sake of administrative convenience, has totally blurred civic outlines. The present book follows the prevailing subjectivity of judgement and includes, or excludes, a particular community simply because it feels, or does not feel, like a 'town'.

In considering the towns that were to be discussed an upper population limit of 25,000 was first envisaged. Such a cut-off would have provided clear working models, for historic towns of up to that size tend to be compact: Ludlow, Richmond and Chichester are excellent examples. It would also have avoided the difficulty of deciding whether or not to include towns inflated by modern industry. And it probably corresponds to the picture of the 'ideal town' in the English imagination.

But there were even stronger disadvantages in imposing such a limit. It would have been necessary to forgo much excellent evidence taken from towns and cities above that size: for example, the dual market-place in Norwich which provides a text-book example of Anglo/Norman polarity; the city walls of York and Chester; the Roman evidence of Colchester, oldest of all our towns. Such a cut-off point, too, would automatically exclude scores of towns which are currently suffering from urban elephantiasis, expanding vastly under technological stimulus. Until the mid-nineteenth century, for example, Nottingham was regarded as being one of the nost beautiful towns in the kingdom. Today, mediaeval Nottingham has been almost wholly digested by nine-teenth- and twentieth-century Nottingham, leaving few physical clues. But there are many examples of large industrialized com-munities whose historic hearts remain essentially unchanged – Jonah in the belly of the whale, as it were. Chester is a good example of these. No formal upper limit is therefore imposed, examples being drawn from whatever community was appropriate although, in general, attention is concentrated on the smaller towns.

The writer of such a book as this has a personal involvement denied the writer of any other kind of book for everybody has to live somewhere. The present author has been fortunate in spending most of his life in three historic, and strongly distinctive, communi-ties: Norwich, Holborn, and Guildford. Holborn is a remarkable survival, an example of the human ability to place its imprint upon the most unpromising environments, retaining identity even under such appalling pressures as exist in central London. It illustrates the fact that London developed by amoebic growth, absorbing independent communities. From 6 P.M. on Friday to 9 A.M. on Monday Holborn returns to the past, belonging again to its citizens with an identity as calm and as clear as that of any cathedral city. It would have been entirely legitimate to take from it examples to illustrate this book. But to have introduced elements from London, or from any other modern megalopolis, would have blurred the story and, with reluctance, this source has been rejected.

It is otherwise with Norwich and Guildford. The two communi-ties provide superb examples of two poles of urban life – the regional capital and the county town. In terms of population, their relative positions have changed over the centuries: at Domesday Norwich was about eight times the size of Guildford, today it is barely three times the size. But their roles remain unchanged: Norwich is still a regional capital, belonging to East Anglia, Guildford a county town, belonging to the four miles or so of countryside that separate it from the next town. Again and again, while seeking examples to illustrate a general trend, the writer has turned instinctively, and in gratitude, to the two communities he has long known and loved.

In one particular matter the writer maintains a deliberate and unrepentant error: the ignoring of the name and boundary changes imposed by the 1974 Local Government Act. In the 1970s the mandarins of Whitehall set about carving up England in the same way that the mandarins of Europe had carved up Africa in the nineteenth century. Just as those 'diplomats' ruled straight lines for hundreds of miles, slicing up ancient tribal unities, so the twentieth-century 'planners' broke up ancient counties, killed off centuries-old names, substituted meaningless bureaucratic labels for names rooted in the soil of history. Rutland disappeared (though sturdily refusing to recognize the fact, as its signposts witness); Swindon vanished, replaced by a suburban entity known as Thamesmead; the ancient Borough of King's Lynn was transformed into something called West Norfolk District Council; in Yorkshire, the noble – and precisely descriptive – name of Riding was thrown on the rubbish heap of history. Town boundaries were immensely widened, dragging in dozens of villages regardless of their traditional affiliations. In Surrey, the village of Ash – physically and socially an all but indistinguishable part of Aldershot – was ceded to Guildford some eight miles away. The ancient, and perfectly clear, term Town Clerk gave way to the pseudo-American Chief Executive.

Partly in a spirit of championship, but mostly in the interests of sheer clarity, this book ignores all such arbitrary changes. Bath, for this book, is where it always has been, in Somerset and not in the river Avon; Rutland maintains its identity, confident in the knowledge that some time in the future some other bureaucratic organization, obsessed with the need to justify its existence, will overturn the work of its predecessor, sowing yet more confusion. The motto for this book might well be that which occurred throughout Leicestershire in the 1970s – 'Rutland Lives!'.

1

The Heritage of Rome

Some time long after the last of the Roman legions had left the shores of Britain, abandoning the country to its fate, a Saxon with the gift of words was travelling through the West Country. There he encountered the ruins of what would be known, centuries later, as Bath and what he saw stirred him so deeply that, Saxon though he was, with all his race's inbred dislike and suspicion of urban life, he recorded what he saw in terms not of triumph but of lament:

Wondrous is this wall stone, broken by fate; the castles are decayed, the work of giants is crumbling. Roofs are fallen, ruinous are the towers, despoiled are the towers with their gates. The grasp of the earth, stout grip of the ground, holds its mighty builders who have perished and gone.

He looked back down the centuries, trying to pierce the veil of the past, recreating in his own terms the culture of that vanished Roman city. 'Bright were the castle dwellings, many the bath-houses, lofty the host of pinnacles, great the tumult of men, many a mead hall full of the joys of men.' Then, on the other side of Europe, there took place movements among peoples of whom he had never heard, movements that made their way to the nerve-endings of the Empire, contracting them. 'Fate the mighty overturns all. The wide walls fell, days of pestilence came. Death swept away all the bravery of men; their forests became waste places. The city fell in ruins . . .'

The physical remains of Roman Britain are extensive in quantity but lacking in quality: the core or foundation of innumerable defensive walls, the foundations of dwelling houses and a few public buildings, some mosaics buried under muddy fields – this is the sum of the physical heritage outside museums. There is nothing in the ex-province of Britain to compare with the theatre at Orange or the Pont du Gard in France, the aqueduct at Segovia in Spain or any of the temples in the lands that once formed the Mediterranean provinces. Hadrian's Wall and the Roman roads are stupendous engineering feats, the latter in particular: but they *are* engineering feats, telling relatively little about the social life of the country.

Nevertheless, despite the poor quality of the remains, for nearly 2000 years the enormous ghost of Rome has brooded over the land to an extent perhaps unequalled anywhere else in Europe, save only Italy. In his *Lettres sur Anglais* Voltaire noted: 'In England the governments of Greece and Rome are the subject of every conversation so that each man is under the necessity of perusing such authors as treat of them and this perusal leads naturally to that of literature.' Long after the Empire had gone to its grave, at one with all the other empires of the past, men like the Saxon minstrel at Bath looked back to the period of its rule with a mixture of nostalgia for its stability and awe at its power, transforming the fact of political and military dominance into myths of supernatural power.

The Romans ran Britain for 400 years. History telescopes time so that the eye slides over the fact that the legions arrived in A.D.43 and left in A.D.410. In real time, it is precisely as though the Spaniards, having successfully landed in 1588 and imposed their culture and language upon the land, should only now, in the 1980s, be preparing to leave. But even this does not give the full impression. The successive waves of conquerors from the Saxons onwards modified an existing civilization. Rome created one, impressing upon the malleable wax of a rural society that pre-eminent Roman creation, the *civitas*. The town. Admittedly, there were already clusters of people in concentration which the British seem to have regarded as resembling a town. In his whirlwind passage across the country Julius Caesar remarked contemptuously 'The Britons call it a town [*oppidum vocant*] when they have occupied woods and fortified ramparts and ditch: they are wont to flock into such places to avoid the inroads of their enemies.' Archaeology has uncovered many such places – Maiden Castle and Hod Hill are two of the most outstanding – but it would be a perverse use of language to give the name 'town', that mysterious fusion of humans, their buildings, laws and artefacts, to these fortified camps. The town was Rome's gift to Britain.

There were two Roman campaigns in Britain. The first, in 55B.C., is the one which every child knows about for it was commanded by that master self-publicist Julius Caesar. His campaign was little more than a raiding party, designed partly to eliminate a nuisance and partly to satisfy that sense of curiosity which is so attractive a part of the man. He returned to Rome, fame and death, leaving the White Island to its own affairs for the next ninety-seven years. But its existence had been noted, and the fact that it possessed some quite useful products; slaves, wheat and tin among them. In A.D.43 the lame, stammering, essentially unheroic but essentially civilized emperor Claudius decided to add the island to the Empire.

His general, Aulus Plautius, landed at Richborough on the Kent coast and fought his way inland to the tribal capital of Camulodun. It was there that Claudius met the army and it was there that the first Roman town was later founded and named, in honour of the emperor, Colonia Claudia Victricensis. The locals, in the time-honoured manner of locals, ignored the pompous official name and simply latinized the old Celtic name and it was as Camulodunum that the city was known until, in due course, the name was transformed into Colchester.

Claudius remained in Britain only sixteen days before, in his turn, returning to Rome and fame and death at the hands of an assassin. But his orders for the imprinting of Rome upon Celtic Britain by the establishment of a city were promptly carried out. In accordance with that custom which bound the Empire together, a vast temple devoted to the worship of the emperor was built. Tacitus described it as the *arx aeternae dominationis* – the 'stronghold of eternal domination' which would stand as symbol of Rome itself in this, Rome's northernmost province. A thousand years later another invader, the Norman, demolished the remains of the vast building to erect an equally large castle but the immense arches of the foundations remain. The Romans had filled them with rammed sand but they were opened up in the seventeenth century and it is possible today to descend and inspect at close quarters the most impressive Roman monument remaining in

Britain. So well did the Romans build, indeed, that not only did the Normans use their work, abutting their own massive masonry to it, but, during World War II, the vaults were used for a purpose that would have seemed magical – or nightmarish – to Romans and Normans alike: as protection from raiders coming by air.

Aulus Plautius used Colchester as his base for the conquest of Britain, dividing his force into three. Legio IX, Hispana, marched northward and in due course founded the town that would be known as Lincoln. Legiones XIV, Gemina, and part of XX, Valeria, went north-westward through the forests of Hertfordshire – Wroxeter marks their goal. Legio II, Augusta, under the second-in-command Vespasian (who would emerge as emperor in his own right) went south-west to the great battle at Maiden Castle: Gloucester was probably born of this campaign. The Fosse Way came into being, the great road running south-west from Lincoln to Bath, acting not only as a line of communication but also as frontier. But it was only a temporary frontier, the legions moving steadily northward and westward until, with the building of Hadrian's Wall in A.D.122, the final shape of Roman Britain had been established.

The purely military structures, like the fort at Hod Hill, and modest market towns, like Caister-by-Norwich, in due course returned to the earth of which they were born, their sites surviving simply as ruins or as nothing more than crop marks. The villas, too, disappeared, the earth hiding their treasures until they were revealed by the spades of archaeologists. But it speaks much for the skill with which the Romans chose the sites for their major towns that, with three exceptions, all those they established in England have survived in some form. The exceptions are Wroxeter and Silchester, which were never reoccupied after being abandoned, and Verulamium – which in effect migrated a few hundred yards uphill and changed its name to St Albans.

Indeed, the very skill of the builders has increased the problems of archaeologists. The ground floors of villas, situated in open country, have survived more or less intact, providing some of the most spectacular mosaics that have survived from Roman Britain. But precisely because the town sites chosen were ideal for urban communities they have been occupied and disturbed century after century, each generation destroying or adapting the work of its predecessors to shape the environment to its own requirements, confusing the archaeological record. It is only in our own time, with the opening up ironically provided by the air raids of World War II, and the large-scale urban 'development' of the post-war years, that large enough areas have been uncovered in the town centres to give an overall picture of the Romano-British town, how it came into being and how it ended.

The clearest picture is provided by Colchester. For over 150 years Britain's oldest town has been in the forefront of the exploration of Roman Britain so that today its museum contains the richest collection of artefacts of the period outside the great collection of the British Museum. Interest was triggered off by the discovery, in 1822, of the eerie statue now known as the Colchester Sphinx. The first archaeologists of the Colchester school were remarkably sophisticated for their day, digging not simply in search of such curios as the statue but also in an attempt to uncover the city buried beneath the modern town. The Norman castle was turned into a museum for housing those finds that were not snapped up by London, and it is this proximity of the finds to their sites of discovery that makes the Colchester collection particularly poignant. The tombstone of Marcus Favonius Facilis – a sombre-faced man firmly clutching his vine-staff of office – stands a few feet vertically above the place where he would have worshipped in life.

It was Mortimer Wheeler who made the first significant discoveries about the buried city. In 1906 the then curator of the museum was eating his sandwich lunch in the grounds just outside the castle. That summer was one of great drought and he noticed a number of cracks in the turf. Preliminary investigation showed that these were caused by the walls of a Roman building. Mortimer Wheeler launched a major excavation in 1920, and as a result of this he advanced the theory – startling then, accepted now – that the so-called 'vaults' under the castle were, in fact, part of the podium of a huge Roman temple, undoubtedly the largest in Britain. Working from this, he produced a conjectural street plan of the Roman town.

Over the following half-century archaeologists extended knowledge of Colchester's Roman past, establishing beyond doubt what had been only advanced theoretically – that Colchester and Colonia Claudia Victricensis, or Camulodunum, were one and the same place. But Colchester is a flourishing modern city and excavations at its heart could take place only in a piecemeal manner. It was not until the late 1970s that opportunity presented itself for the investigation of a relatively large central area. This was the development of a modern shopping centre to be known as the Culver Street Precinct. The precinct would cover two acres – or approximately one fiftieth of the ground area of the Roman city – and its basement would go down twenty-five feet. As it was known that the archaeological remains occupied only the upper ten feet it was imperative to carry out an investigation before they were finally and utterly destroyed. The owners of the site proved co-operative and the Colchester Archaeological Trust under its director, Phillip Crummy, undertook the massive dig.

Among the finds was evidence of an immense and widespread fire. In his report for July, 1981, Phillip Crummy wrote:

Floors were scorched all over bright red and black in intense heat. In many places, bases of daub walls survived in place as bright red stumps sealing strips of charcoal that were all that survived of their timber frames ... To the inhabitants of that time, the full horror of the event would have defied description: to the modern archaeologist, the holocaust presents a marvellous opportunity to examine the remains of buildings not only preserved to an extraordinary degree but also dated.

The holocaust so graphically described was the result of the British rebellion of A.D.60/61 when the Iceni, under their queen Boadicea (or Boudicca), swept down from the north putting Colchester, St Albans and London to the flames. The Culver Street excavation substantiates Tacitus's claim that the town was totally destroyed.

The Boadicean fire enables the birth of Colchester as a town, as distinct from a legionary fortress, to be dated with remarkable precision. It is known from historical sources that the remains of the XXth Legion were transferred from Colchester to South Wales in A.D.48, leaving the fortress empty. Twelve years later the Iceni found a flourishing community at Colchester upon which to wreak their vengeance – contemporary reports say that 70,000 people were slaughtered in the three towns and, though the number was undoubtedly exaggerated, equally undoubtedly the population of Colchester must have been in the hundreds or even thousands. The town therefore came into being during the twelve years between the departure of the legion and the arrival of Boadicea's horde. What evidently happened was that, instead of the now unused fortress being demolished, the base was converted into a town by demolishing the military defences and adapting the existing buildings – in particular the barrack blocks – to civilian use. The town was rebuilt after the fire but never recovered its earlier importance, yielding precedence to such rising places as London, Lincoln and York but retaining beneath its mediaeval and modern streets the secret of a community's transition from military fortress to civilian town.

The strength of the Roman army was its technique of standardiz-ation, a fact of immense help to the student of Roman Britain for the description of one site can stand for dozens. The heart of the legionary fortress was the *principia* or headquarters building, consisting of a courtyard surrounded by a colonnade and leading to a cross-hall that could hold the entire garrison standing shoulder to shoulder. Somewhere in this cross-hall would be the tribunal, a small, raised platform from whence the commanding officer could address the entire force. Accidentally or otherwise, the site of the *principia* frequently remained the heart of the town which grew out of the fortress: in York the minster stands exactly over the old Roman headquarters building; Chester's cathedral is within the circuit of the fortress.

Adjoining the *principia* is the *praetorium*, the commander's house, and on its other side is the vital part of the whole – the granaries. Behind this central headquarters area is the barrack-block, destined to become the first civilian residences of the town.

Two or sometimes three main roads divide the fortress into four or six major sections. The road from the *principia* to the main front gate is, invariably, known as the *via praetoria* while that running back from the headquarters building to the corresponding back gate is, also invariably, the *via decumana*. The road crossing at right angles in front of the *principia*, connecting the two side gates, is the *via principalis*.

Of all that remains of Rome in Britain, the relics of these four roads and their corresponding gate-sites are the most persistent, the most evident. Long after their origins had been forgotten, they remained to govern the shape of the future town. In York, the *via principalis* and the *via praetoria* survive unequivocally under their mediaeval names of Stonegate and Petergate: in Chester, Eastgate Street is the Roman *via principalis* and Northgate the *via decumana*. By a happy chance, Chester's nineteenth-century town hall was built almost on the site of the *principia* so that the modern Northgate Street runs beside the modern headquarters building exactly as the *via decumana* ran beside the Roman administrative centre. And even though the physical gates have, in the majority of cases, long since disappeared, the gaps in the city walls remain to dictate the direction of the internal streets. Today, the little city of Chichester provides probably the clearest working model of the Roman town plan, for city walls, gate-sites and streets all survive as a linked unit. Lincoln can provide the remarkable spectacle of a Roman gateway still surviving, still used by traffic. The Newport Arch, spanning what was Ermine Street and is now the A15 to Hull, became a victim of its own efficiency in 1964 when it was rammed by a lorry passing through it. Meticulously restored, it remains the only Roman gate in Britain used for its original purpose, although the road level has risen by eight feet, giving it a somewhat squat appearance. Colchester's Balkerne Gate, the only other surviving Roman gate in Britain, is far more impressive although, being in a cul-de-sac, it lacks the dynamic character of Lincoln's. Its modern name indicates that it was once blocked (Balkerne derives from 'baulk'), and this blockage is the main reason for its survival. Originally it was the west gate of Camulodunum, leading directly into the heart of the town along what is now the High Street, and it was probably blocked as a defensive measure at the beginning of the Saxon period, a significant indication of the chaos that followed the rule of Rome. Its origins were forgotten – as late as the nineteenth century it was assumed to be a fort – and by the time it was identified and uncovered it was the sole survivor of the city gates, all others having been demolished as hindrances to traffic. It would have been built in the standard manner with two central carriageways for wheeled traffic and two smaller pedestrian tunnels, one on either side. The main central arch and the northern pedestrian way have disappeared, but the tunnel on the south side survives, together with the lower part of the guard house. The twentieth-century pedestrian can therefore follow in the footsteps of his predecessor of sixteen hundred years ago.

Colchester and Lincoln provide the most starkly dramatic examples of town gates: during excavations in Lincoln in 1970 the foundations of two more gates were discovered, the East Gate and the massive West Gate now straddled by the modern municipal buildings. York, Chester and Chichester provide the clearest examples of the orientation of streets. But all towns founded by Rome bear evidence of their ancestry – Winchester, Bath, Gloucester and Canterbury in particular showing the gates and main highways even after the bombing of World War II and redevelopments of the post-war years. The city walls survive in a surprising number of towns to give the 'feel' of the Roman town to anyone walking round them. The Roman walls of Dorchester contained the entire town until the nineteenth century; Colchester's walls, built after the Boadicean rebellion are intact along the greater part of their circumference. The modern inner ring road, indeed, passing below the mighty Balkerne Gate, enables the twentieth-century motorist to see, fleetingly, what the third-century horseman would have seen gradually disclosing itself. Parts of the city walls of York, and even more of Chester's, have Rome as foundation so that, in walking along these walls, one is walking at approximately the same height as that at which the legionaries would have walked.

The Romans founded three types of town, colonies, tribal capitals and a single *municipium* – Verulamium. Colonies were – quite literally – colonies, miniature Rome set down in hostile lands, initially occupied by veterans and discharged soldiers. There were four in Britain – Colchester, Lincoln, Gloucester and York – and the reason for their foundation was succinctly summed up by Tacitus in his description of Colchester as 'a strong colony [*colonia*] of ex-soldiers on conquered territory to provide a protection against rebels – and a centre for instructing the provincials in the procedures of the law': in other words, to show the barbarians how Rome managed things. The tribal capitals reflected the pre-Roman organization of the country, the Romans, as ever quick to adopt local customs to their advantage, employing the tribal system as an instrument of local government. Thus Durovernum of the tribe of the Cantii came into being, in due course changing its name to Canterbury; Venta Belgarum – the market of the Belgae – became Winchester and survived to become England's capital; while Venta Icenorum became Caister-by-Norwich and returned in due course to its native elements. Chicester, Silchester, Exeter, Leicester, Wroxeter and Dorchester were among these capitals. The *municipium* of Verulamium, was unusual in that although it resembled a colony in all details it was not in fact founded by Rome but already existed and received its constitution by grant.

The size of the towns varied from Silchester, with barely 100 acres (40 ha), to London with 330 (135 ha). The population of the smaller tribal capitals would have been perhaps 2000: a larger town such as Verulamium might have numbered 6000 at its peak. The standard of living was high. The Roman obsession with cleanliness is well demonstrated not only by the ubiquitous bath-house, but also by the sewerage system, examples of which have been found in Lincoln, Bath, St Albans and York. Nothing resembling the monumental aqueducts of Latin Europe is to be found in Britain but the water supply to the towns was highly sophisticated. The water supply for Lincoln came from a source a mile and a half away and was brought up to the town under pressure along an underground water main of earthenware pipes encased in concrete, and stored in a reservoir behind the north wall. The supply for Dorchester was brought along an open channel, following the natural contours. Public lavatories were a commonplace: they were based on the standard military design of which the one showing the clearest method of operation is at Housesteads on Hadrian's Wall. An open sewer of stone was covered with wooden seats, and was flushed periodically. In front of the users was a narrow channel, containing clean running water for the cleansing of the sponges employed. Two large stone basins contained water for washing the hands. It is indubitable that this vital, elementary service was not again provided to a similar standard until the twentieth century.

By one of the quirks of time, the most outstanding survival in the tribal capital of Wroxeter is a great, raw ruin known colloquially as the Old Work. It is the remains of the bath-house. Its survival could be regarded as emblematic, for the bath-house was the very emblem of Roman civilization: certainly, no important town in England was without this complex that combined hygiene with social intercourse. The distinctive hypocaust is to be found at every important site. Usually they are in ruins, but in a basement below a shop in Chester's Bridge Street is one that has survived intact, together with the cold bath – not much larger than a modern bath – hewn out of the living rock.

Pre-eminent among these baths, and undoubtedly rivalled only by Hadrian's Wall in modern popular fame, is the thermal house at Bath. It predated even the Romans, who named the town after the native goddess Sul to whom the waters were sacred, rather than impose their own name upon it – even though they identified Sul with Minerva. The town, as Aquae Sulis, played the same role in Romano-British society – at once therapeutic and social – that it was to play in modern society from the eighteenth century onwards.

Aquae Sulis was a tiny town, the circuit of the walls less than three-quarters of a mile all told. At its heart was the sacred spring, daily pumping out – as it still does – a quarter of a million gallons of mineral water at a temperature of 120°F (49°C). Around the spring were the social and religious establishments associated with it – the temple of Sul Minerva, the thermal baths and probably a theatre. This ceremonial heart suffered – or benefited – from the same fate, though on a tiny scale, as that which overtook Herculaneum for it was eventually engulfed by mud and so preserved for centuries. The spring lies in a little hollow and when the complex drainage system broke down in the early fifth century the water collected, forming a marsh. Over the following centuries the level of the marsh rose as the surrounding buildings toppled into it, and in attempts to make a solid footing successive generations laid successive floorings above it until, in due course, the complex was buried twelve feet deep. The Thermae were rediscovered in 1755 but it was not until 1878 that excavations revealed the full extent of the bathing establishment. In 1981 a two-year co-ordinated excavation was launched to uncover the temple and, in the sober words of the archaeological report: 'The excavations produced remarkable and unexpected results.' Twelve feet below street level the Roman precinct floor was discovered 'perfectly preserved beneath a mass of black mud and rubble'. Further excavations provided evidence as to how the Romans had tackled the problem of containing the spring 'involving the ramming of hundreds of oak piles into the mud before beginning their enclosure wall'. Thousands of votive offerings were found in a layer of sand – the Romans obeying the same impulse to throw coins into the water as any modern tourist faced with a fountain. 'They still lay in splendid condition – between ten and twenty thousand coins, curses written on sheets of pewter, silver vessels from the treasury.' The altar erected to the goddess Sul Minerva by a temple haruspex, Lucius Marcius Memor, that had been discovered during a tribal excavation in 1965, was set up on its original site in March 1982.

It is the immediacy of Bath that accounts for its enormous attraction – the knowledge that this is the 'same' water as bathed the limbs of veteran soldiers, elegant young women and grizzled civil servants who died centuries before the Norsemen left Scandinavia. The modern tourist and the sixth-century Saxon poet share the same sensation as they watch the steaming water gushing out of its depths: 'Stone courts stood here: the stream with its great gush sprang forth hotly: the wall enclosed all within its bright bosom . . .'

The theatre of Bath probably lies under the abbey and so is unlikely ever to be brought to light. But it would have been built to the same plan, and probably the same dimensions, as that at Verulamium. Although discovered in 1847 Verulamium's was not excavated until 1934 and is the only visible Roman theatre in Britain. Unwary visitors tend to believe that the high grassy bank circling the complex is part of it whereas it is, in fact, simply the spoil removed. But from this high bank it is possible to get a bird's-eye view of the whole. The first theatre, built some time after A.D.155, had only a small wooden stage, but subsequent rebuilding in A.D.200 and 300 enlarged and elaborated the whole complex. Looking down upon these waist-high remains is to be reminded forcibly that the Romans were as insular as the British in transplanting throughout their Empire customs and buildings to which they were accustomed, no matter how uncongenial the environment. The British introducing bacon and eggs and tennis into Malaya were no more eccentric than the Romans introducing oysters – and an unroofed theatre in a land that was to become notorious for the unpredictability of its climate.

Traditionally, the ending of Roman Britain is shown as an act of high drama with shaggy barbarians racing in with swords and flaming torches, destroying what they could not understand. It is a picture given apparent substance by the famous discovery, in the remains of the hypocaust at Wroxeter, of the skeleton of an old man with a bag of coins near his hand. The manner of his death seemed straight from a Hollywood epic – the terrified old man crawling beneath the floor of his house, clutching his life savings, with Teutonic fiends carousing drunkenly overhead, while he gradually suffocated.

But whatever the reason for, or the manner of, the death of the Roman citizen of Wroxeter, it cannot be taken as symbolic of the death of Roman Britain. The ending was far slower, far less dramatic and far more poignant. In A.D.410 the legions were withdrawn to defend Italy – then itself simply an outpost of an Empire whose capital was in the Middle East since the transference of power to Constantinople. Nine years later Emperor Honorius gave 'permission' to the towns of Roman Britain to defend themselves – in other words, he let it be known pretty clearly that they could expect no help from either Constantinople or Rome. Rome itself was dying, the mother city descending into a catatonic trance that would last until the fourteenth century.

In Britain, the life slowly ebbed away. Tantalizing fragments of archaeology, brief references in sparse contemporary chronicles suggested that the process took nearly two centuries. The forum at Cirencester was still heavily in use until at least A.D.430 – a generation after the legions had gone. The water system was working in St Albans throughout the century. In A.D.446 the towns of Britain were still sufficiently civilized to communicate with each other and speak with a common voice, addressing a final desperate plea for help to a distant, helpless Mediterranean administration.

But even this was not the end. The *Anglo-Saxon Chronicle* has the most tantalizing hint of all in a bald entry for the year A.D.577, saying simply that in that year the West Saxons killed three British kings and captured 'three of their cities – Gloucester, Cirencester and Bath'. One hundred and seventy years after the official abandonment by Rome, three of their cities were still recognized as such by barbarians.

But after that the darkness descends, finally.

2

The Birth of England

King Arthur, if such a person existed, fell at the battle of Camlann about the year A.D.515. Whether or not he was a real person, or simply a personification of civilization fighting against the engulfing force of barbarism, the date assigned to his death can usefully be taken as marking the effective end of Roman England. From this point onwards, the land belonged neither to Celt nor to Latin but to Germanic tribes. And the first of them, the Saxons, in the words of Tacitus 'regarded towns as the defence of slavery and the grave of freedom'. Nearly four centuries were to pass before the town again became a dynamic factor of English life, stimulated by the Danish invasions of the ninth century.

What happened to the Roman towns in that long interval? Did they die, or merely go into hibernation?

Evidence for continuity between Roman and 'English' England is tantalizingly indirect, obscure. The physical remains are everywhere evident, but the survival of a hypocaust or street alignment no more provides evidence of urban continuity than does the existence of Stonehenge provide evidence of religious continuity from Bronze Age Britain. Yet the towns are there – in due course, unlike Stonehenge, they flowered again. York emerged in the seventh century as the capital of Northumbria: as early as A.D.601 Pope Gregory chose it as the state of England's second archbishopric. At least three of its churches are built directly over Roman buildings. There was a royal palace in London, built over – perhaps emerging from – the Roman Cripplegate Fort. Does all this constitute genuine continuity, in the sense that the present, existing cathedral at Canterbury is the direct, true descendant of the humble church probably built in A.D.602?

It is difficult today to get that idea of total desolation which so stirred the Saxon minstrel in Bath, for the towns have either been incorporated into busy modern cities, or their remains sterilized by archaeologists. Silchester in Berkshire is one of the few which probably looks today much as it did in the sixth century. It was never reoccupied for it had an inadequate water-supply. The Romans had sited it for political reasons and their urban organiz-ation was efficient enough to keep it supplied with water: when that organization collapsed, the water-supply failed and the town died completely. The central area was excavated in the nineteenth century, but filled in again. The great walls survive around most of the perimeter, in some places as high as fifteen feet. In the south-west corner the original earthworks rise to over twenty feet. Along this section the forces of nature have almost triumphed over the works of man, with tree roots thrusting deep into the vitals of the walls, the earthworks thickly covered with shrubs and trees so that the path along the dry moat winds through a species of wood. In 1981 excavations began in the great amphitheatre situated, as were most such structures, outside the town. Doubtless in due course the busy savants of the Department of the Environment will strip the mound of its rather sinister-looking holly trees, baring the remains and effectively dispelling the ghosts but, at the time of writing, it probably looks much as the Saxon minstrel might have seen it: 'the grasp of the earth, stout grip of the ground' pulling even Rome low.

Not all the towns were wholly abandoned like this. The 1980s excavation in Colchester provided evidence of a few poor Saxon huts. But the entire Roman street-pattern of the town was destroyed in the ninth or tenth century during a major replanning of Colchester which left only the walls and the gateways. But even when, in due course, life returned, the newcomers rarely made use of the existing street-patterns. The two main streets, the *via principalis* and the *via praetoria/decumana* might well survive, but not because the newcomers wanted to build along them. The streets were aligned with the gateways and it was obviously far easier to enter and leave the town by the gate-openings than by scrambling over the walls. Post-war excavations in Winchester produce a curious picture if the grid of the Saxon street system is laid over that of the Roman. The two systems coincide only at one place – along the main east-west axis. Even allowing for the fact that the debris would have accumulated in the streets, would it not have been easier – and safer – to have cleared them and erected new structures on the foundations of the Roman street walls? Instead, the newcomers preferred to level off the debris and build upon it. In Chester, a local solution of the problem probably produced the beautiful and enigmatic Rows. No definitive solution has been advanced to account for this unique urban feature but it is supposed that the first-floor walkways probably represent a pathway over the massive remains of Roman buildings lining the street. In due course, the street would have been cleared, opening up those sites not occupied by street-level shops. Certainly the Rows exist only within the limits of the fortress.

The presence of substantial Roman foundations was by no means welcome to all later builders, particularly if their structure was on a different alignment. This happened at York where the builders of the minster found the foundations of the *principia* an embarrassment. The ground there was of different load-bearing capabilities and the presence of the massive Roman foundations could well have broken the back of their own structure. The master mason at York solved the problem by building a timber arch over the obstruction.

But although evidence of continuity can be adduced here and there, in general the withdrawal of the legions created a break, a dislocation, the urban impulse – where it survived – tending to be directed in other channels. Ironically the most powerful evidence of what might be called psychic continuity – the continuance of the human spirit in a particular locality rather than the mere survival of cemented stone – is provided by one of Rome's victims. In A.D.209 a Roman citizen of Verulamium called Alban was condemned to death for refusing to sacrifice to the emperor. He was not only a citizen, but also probably a soldier of high rank and so was entitled to death by the sword instead of one of the more grisly, protracted terminations provided by Rome for enemies of the state. He was taken out of the city and on to the beautiful green hill that lay behind it and there beheaded. A late sixth-century narrative describes the hill as it was about the year A.D.583 when the writer visited it. The writer makes Alban and the usual ghoulish crowd leave Verulamium: 'They climbed the hill which rose with inexpressible beauty for five hundred paces from the Theatre. It was clothed and coloured with various kinds of flowers.' In due course, a rough shrine appeared over or near the site of the execution and this, in turn, gave way to the immense abbey – much of it built of bricks taken from Verulamium – which became the focal point of the new town of St Albans.

But though the towns might have entered a hibernation so deep that it resembled death, the roads survived. It is an experience both disorientating and salutary to superimpose a road map of Roman Britain over a road map of the modern country. Disorientating because the eye follows a road expecting it to lead to a currently important town and finds, instead, some utterly obscure village: Watling Street and the great Fosse Way cross at a place called Venonae, today simply a point on the map known as High Cross. But the experience is salutary, too, because it is truly extraordinary how many of the roads have been transformed into modern highways, and how many of the important Roman points along them are important modern towns. Watling Street demonstrates this unequivocally. Starting at Dover, it goes on through Canterbury, Chatham, Rochester and London as the A2, then on through St Albans as the A5 – though ending in the now small village of Wroxeter. The oldest of them all, the Fosse Way, links Lincoln, Newark and Leicester as the A46 before continuing on to Bath under various names but all identifiable as the one artery. The continuance of the roads ensured that, sooner or later, the towns they had once served would come to life again. The Saxons might despise the towns, but they made use of the roads even though they sited their own villages well away from them.

War, trade, and religion were to provide the stimuli both for the revival of Roman towns and the founding of the first English towns. And the greatest of these stimuli was war.

In A.D.789, the *Anglo-Saxon Chronicle* records, three Danish ships put in at Portland. The reeve of Dorchester, in whose jurisdiction the port fell, arrived to enquire their business and was killed by them, the first recorded victim of the Vikings. For the next century they ravaged the eastern half of England, their invasions gradually changing from sporadic raids to organized military campaigns. By the year A.D.871 they were firmly established throughout East Anglia and Northumbria. For these Scandinavians, who used England's rivers to penetrate deep into England's heart, were not only skilled seamen and killers. They were, willy-nilly, town builders. Or, at least, their curious mode of life made desirable some means of defending themselves when not actually engaged in rapine. As seamen, they realized the need for, and were accustomed to, acting as a unit and by applying that maritime discipline to the practical needs of defence, they evolved highly efficient fortifications. Curiously, these people so very different from the Romans developed much of the same technique for ensuring their safety in a hostile foreign land by building a fort and ensuring that it was adequately garrisoned. They established themselves in two Roman towns, Lincoln and Leicester, and three Anglo-Saxon villages – Nottingham, Stamford, and Derby.

Opposing these dynamic seafarers were their reluctant host/victims, the static Anglo-Saxon farmers. These, with the powerful plough evolved in the heavy lands of their country of origin, had literally carved out a way of life for themselves away from the lighter lands colonized by the Romans and their protégés. It is in these Saxon villages that true continuity must be sought between undocumented past and recorded history, a continuity created by the simple, square stone churches that they built. The Saxon church of Escomb in Northumbria was used as a place of worship from the time that it was built, in the late eighth century, until the building of the parish church in the late nineteenth century. The little gem of a church in Bradford-on-Avon has an even more imposing length of time attached to it. Writing in 1125 William of Malmesbury claimed that it had been founded by St Anselm himself. But Anselm died in 1109 and modern archaeology places at least the lower half of the church in the early eighth century, certainly a generation before that of Escomb. In the nineteenth century part of it was turned into a school and part into a cottage, but it has now been reconsecrated and serves, more than twelve hundred years after it was built, its original purpose.

Though the Anglo-Saxons might prefer to go about their business of farming and worshipping, they were also perfectly ready to reverse the traditional process and turn their ploughshares into swords. And under their king Alfred – one of the few kings really to deserve that title of Great which historians freely bestow upon monarchs – they threw themselves into the task first of containing, then of pushing back, the invading seamen from the north. Alfred's strategy was that employed by all great commanders – copy the enemy's best weapon and improve it. The Danes' most efficient weapon was discipline as embodied in their standing army and in their fortified camps. Alfred adopted both: the fortified camp – *burh* in Saxon – became the town of the future, even while its name, anglicized into 'borough' was to become part of the language of municipal affairs, given greater prominence by the municipal reforms of the nineteenth century.

Looking back over Alfred's life his biographer, Asser, heaped praise upon him for his town-building activities:

What shall I say of the cities and towns that he restored, and of the others he had built where none stood before? Of the buildings marvellously wrought with gold and silver under his direction. Of the royal halls and chambers, wonderfully built of stone and wood at his command.

Alfred's contribution was great, but not unprecedented. The Saxons were already well acquainted with the means of fortifying a position – the fact that a common noun existed for such a place is ample proof. An area was enclosed with a ditch, an earthen rampart and a stockage with four gates. Alfred took the basic design, expanded it, though leaving room for local adaptations, and created a chain of forts so that no village in his jurisdiction was more than twenty miles from a fort. An invaluable document of about A.D. 919, called the Burghal Hidage, lists these *burhs*, enabling us to identify accurately those which evolved into towns. The name of the document indicates the means whereby the building and the manning of the forts were financed: each 'hide' or measurement of land had to provide one man, or a monetary equivalent of the work he could do.

The Hidage lists thirty-three *burhs*. Some were simply Iron Age forts – these returned to ruin after the military threat passed. Others were established in the abandoned Roman towns – Bath, Winchester and Chichester for example. But others again were either totally new foundations, or developed villages – places like Shaftesbury, Malmesbury and Southwark. Exactly like the siting of pill-boxes in World War II, the primary choice of their sites was

military and in the first urgent years of the Danish threat little
attention was paid to any secondary value that the sites might
possess. But after the year A.D.920, not only were no more new
burhs established, but existing ones began to be assessed in
terms of their potential economic value as trading centres. The
economically useless *burhs* were gradually abandoned in favour of
places that could combine defence with trade. Thus the function
of Eashing, near Godalming in Surrey, was transferred to Guildford, which had the added advantage of being at the junction of a
major road system; in Devon, Totnes took over from Halwell and
Barnstaple from Pilton for similar reasons. Those *burhs* which did
not have the advantage of trading potential withered away or
remained as villages. In Somerset, for instance, Alfred had established *burhs* at Lyng, Langport and Axbridge to guard that island
of Athelney which had stood him in such good stead when he was
in hiding from the Danes. But while they were in good military
situations, they were not on trade routes and today all three are
small villages. Similar considerations applied to the Roman towns
that were refortified: Portchester returned to the fields after a brief
renaissance as a Saxon fort.

The establishment of the Danelaw in A.D.878 did not bring the
long struggle to an end, but it did define spheres of influence
which were to have long-term effects on both the physical and the
social pattern of English towns. Alfred forced a division of England
with a line running diagonally from Chester to London, the Danes
remaining north-east of that line, the Saxons south-west. The first
king of all England, Edgar, ascended the throne in A.D.959, but by
then Danish customs had permeated the lives of all those in the
north-east, adding yet another strand to the fabric of town life.

The Church continued the process. In choosing sites for their
first cathedrals the bishops, as heirs of Rome, were predisposed in
favour of Roman sites. Five of the first seven sees were adminis-
tered from Roman towns: Saint Augustine established his two
metropolitan sees in London and York in A.D.601, and Canterbury,
Rochester and Winchester were added by the middle of the
century. Only two sees in this early period were of non-Roman
foundation – those of Dunwich and Lichfield. But the sites of
many cathedrals changed, the dioceses expanding and contracting

as the bishops adjusted their administrative areas in accordance with social changes. On the eve of the Norman Conquest, which gave the dioceses a final shape except for later minor adjustments, there were fifteen dioceses of which five no longer exist, including those of Dorchester-on-Thames, Elmham in Norfolk, Sherborne in Dorset and Ramsbury in Wiltshire.

Only one urban Saxon cathedral has been archaeologically investigated and that is at Winchester where a building approximately 100 feet long (less than one-fifth the length of the present cathedral), built about the year A.D.648, was uncovered during the excavations in 1970. The presumption is that most of the others lie buried deep beneath the foundations of their mediaeval successors and, apart from fragmentary investigations during the course of repairs and maintenance of the present buildings, an overall picture is unlikely to emerge of these early precursors. The Church, again, tended to choose a Roman town as the site for that characteristic institution, the monastery: Gloucester and Bath were to owe much of their revival to the presence in their midst of monastic foundations. Elsewhere, their enormous wealth and power either virtually created towns, or stimulated their development to a remarkable degree.

By the end of the tenth century, all the creative elements of the English town – Romano-British, Saxon, Angle, Jute, Danish, ecclesiastical – were at work in the land, awaiting only the vast impress of the Norman Conquest to anneal them into one. It was this racial variegation which was to give the richness to the urban pattern. The shape of the Roman town was imposed from above; the English town grew by accretion. If by some miracle the Roman towns had survived unchanged we should probably find them dullish sorts of places – forum here, basilica there, bath-house of such and such a shape, walls of such and such a height and width – very much like the mass-produced commercial architecture of our own day.

If Colchester can stand as a good example of the first Roman towns, another East Anglian town – Norwich – can stand as an example of the town developing by accretion. At one stage, academics debated whether or not Norwich was originally the Venta Icenorum, the market-town of the tribe of Iceni who destroyed Colchester. Folk memory insisted that the place known as Caister-by-Norwich, not Norwich, was the Venta and embodied that memory in a doggerel couplet:

> Caister was a city when Norwich was none
> Norwich was built with Caister's stone.

Folk memory distorts, but never invents. It is highly improbable that the builders of Norwich would have carted stone three or four miles from Caister when they had, beneath their feet, ample supplies of handsome, easily accessible material – flint. But academic opinion now follows popular belief and gives the accolade to Caister as the earlier, Roman foundation.

One of the guides through the richly chaotic founding period is that of place-names. There is a Ber Street in Norwich and, bearing in mind that the Saxons invariably referred to a Roman road as 'strete', it needs no great feat of translation to deduce that 'Berstrete' is a Roman road relating to a *burh*. Norwich was evidently important enough for the Romans to drive one – and possibly more – of their roads near or through the site. The road ascends a hill, taking the idyllic name of Bracondale, but at the top it takes on that name of Ber Street. In the 1930s it suffered the same fate as so many of our ancient town centres and became a slum: even today it is a depressing sight, with the gaps created by air raids now devoted to car parks, dumps and the like. But the street is of broad and handsome proportions, running along a ridge high above the river Yare, leading straight as a dart into what would become the heart of the city.

Place-names provide further clues. Two of the oldest wards in Norwich, lying one on either side of the city, are Conesford and Coslany. Both were Anglian foundations, the former situated on or controlling the 'king's ford', the latter situated on an ey or island. In due course, Conesford became the Saxon *burh*, but Coslany survived and flourished as the 'leet over the water' – the district on the other side of the river. Other, small, settlements came into being, among them one still known as Westwick, distinguishing it from that other *wic*, or trading place, in the north, Northwick, which would eventually give its name to the whole complex.

'Norwich' enters written history with an act of violence. In the year 1002, the *Anglo-Saxon Chronicle* records, 'Swegen came with his fleet to Northwic and wasted and burned the burh.' It was, nevertheless, the compatriots of the destroyer Swegen who next put their imprint on the growing town. It became part of the Danelaw and so subject to Danish control. Place-names, again, provide additional clues. Street-names like Pottergate, Fishergate, Westlegate indicate not city-gates but 'ways' or 'streets', derived from the same source as the word 'gait', a literary term in the south but one still used colloquially in the north. Norwich, with its easy access to the North Sea via the river Yare and its central position in rich farming land, became one of the major centres of the Danelaw. The Danes settled down within comfortable reach of the river, turned to trade with the same skill and vigour with which they turned to piracy, and developed their own area around the market-place that would be known as Tombland. Place-names science is full of traps: more than one unwary writer has built up a macabre background of Tombland (burial place for victims of the Black Death is prime favourite) although the word is simply the Danish for 'open space' (*toomlond*). It was the effective heart of the town by the time the Normans arrived and they, in their turn, established yet another centre, the market place beneath their great castle known as Mancroft (from *magna croft*, the big field). In 1096 Bishop Herbert de Losinga decided to move his cathedral from Thetford to Norwich and established a monastery abutting Tombland to serve it. By the opening of the twelfth century, therefore, Norwich could be regarded almost as a federation of half a dozen little townships waiting to be made into one. Such, too, was the condition of England at the dawn of its true nationhood.

3

The Shaping of the Town

Although the detecting of differences between the town and the village must be almost entirely subjective, there is nevertheless one constant factor, one true difference, between all towns, and all villages. In its initial founding stage the town is an act of somebody's conscious will: somebody, somewhere had to say 'there will be a town here' and thereafter act, or enjoin action, upon that decision. The village, by contrast, is self-planted, developing out of the need to work the land. If certain factors are present, then it will turn into a town; if not, it will remain as a village or wither away entirely. And the factors are topographical.

Pre-eminent among all the factors was the river. The English treat the urban sections of their rivers very badly indeed. Bath is one of the few towns to make a central feature of its river, providing a feeling of space and excitement almost at the town centre. The little town of Wisbech in Cambridgeshire, too, gives pride of place to the river that runs through it. The handsome Georgian houses are ranged facing each other on each side of the Nene, giving a decidedly unEnglish look to the place: its citizens are fond of comparing it with Venice but it more resembles one of the Dutch towns which so proudly dominate the waters they have tamed. The city of Bedford, too, has provided a handsome river-side walk and parts of York are best seen from the Ouse. But in most other towns and cities, even quite small ones and those with honourable records of town-planning, the river is, at best, relegated to a pretty additional feature used for occasional recreation or, far worse and far more often, is turned into a ditch with ugly blank walls on either side. In part, this is a legacy of the Industrial Revolution: heavy goods – coal, builders' material and the like – were cheaply transported by water and the warehouses and dumps to receive them grew up, forcing the town to turn its back on the source of its being.

In town after town, the river is seen as the womb of urban life.

Silchester died because it had no river and the life of Old Sarum in Wiltshire was substantially shortened by the same fact. The site was a natural fortress and was used as such by Romans, Saxons and Normans, drawing their water from wells. So attractive was it that it became the seat of a bishopric in 1075 and the cathedral was built there twenty years later. But the builders, unwisely, had not questioned why the Saxons had christened the place *Searobyrg* or 'dry town'. The water-supply which had proved adequate for a military site proved wholly inadequate for a growing town. This, together with the cramped, claustrophobic nature of the place, spelled its end. In 1227 the bishop moved his cathedral down to the lush water-meadows of the Avon and New Sarum – Salisbury – came into being leaving Old Sarum to become a scandal, centuries later, as a rotten borough.

The river provided the first obvious need – water – and a substantial amount of protein in the form of fish. But it also provided transport and energy. Until the eighteenth century water transport was not only easier but immensely cheaper than that by road. When Walter Frost, master of the cathedral works at Winchester in 1532, wanted a load of gypsum he got a ton of it from Paris (hence its name, plaster of Paris). He found that it cost him exactly the same, three shillings and fourpence, to shift the load by water from Paris to Southampton as it did to bring it the twelve miles by road from Southampton to Winchester. King's Lynn owed its prosperity to the fact that it was situated at the seaward end of a riverine network that spread through the Midlands. The all-powerful Hanseatic League chose the little town as one of its depots in England primarily for that reason.

Inland ports were accordingly significant. Gainsborough in Lincolnshire was well established as such on the Trent by the thirteenth century. George Eliot used it as the model for St Ogg's in *The Mill on the Floss* – 'a venerable town with the red-fluted roofs and the broad warehouse gables where the black ships unlade themselves of their burthens from the far north, and carry away in exchange, the precious inland products, the well crushed cheese and the soft fleeces'. The vital role of rivers in urban life is well demonstrated by contrasting the development of Winchester, England's old capital, with London, the one remaining a small town on a little river; the other, at the mouth of Britain's largest river, expanding into one of the great cities of the world.

And until the introduction of steam-power with the Industrial Revolution, the hydraulic power of the rivers provided the only alternative to muscle-power in towns. In 1580 there were twenty-five obstructions of one form and another – weirs, locks, mills – in the twenty-five miles between Abingdon in Berkshire and Maidenhead.

The river provided water, transport and power: the land itself provided protection. Those towns sited with military defence in mind are more likely to belong to the turbulent Saxon period than to the Roman – with its confidence in the shield of the legion – or the post-Norman period, with its relative stability. Shaftesbury in Dorset is a superb example of a town founded primarily with defence in mind. The site is a sandstone spur rearing up some 700 feet above sea level on three sides while descending at a gentle gradient on its north-eastern side. Here a *burh* was established at the end of the ninth century. Like Old Sarum, it had no adequate water-supply and entered into a complicated arrangement with a village in the valley below to use its springs. To retain the right, a custom grew up whereby the mayor and townsfolk descended the hill in the annual Byzant ceremony – a custom still enacted (see page 117). Shaftesbury was dependent upon water brought up laboriously by hand or on horseback until as late as 1615 – an excellent indication of the attraction of defence over domestic comfort. Unlike Old Sarum it did not outgrow its needs and so survived as a town – but few of these hill towns wholly outgrew the limitations imposed upon them and most remained relatively small.

Durham is another foundation where disadvantages of site from a civil point of view were offset by its immensely strong military position on a bluff towering above the river Wear and surrounded by it on three sides. The founders of Shrewsbury were attracted by the fact that the river Severn made an immense loop: they and their descendants improved on nature by digging ditches that almost converted the site into an island. Where Shaftesbury had too little water, Shrewsbury had too much, being frequently flooded – a fact which helped to limit its growth. Ely, in the Fenland, was similarly affected. The 'Isle of Ely' was ground rising a few feet above the surrounding fens and connected to dry land by a causeway which was always being flooded. That indefatigable traveller Celia Fiennes was particularly caustic about Ely. She seems to have visited it in the winter of 1697 when, as usual, the causeway was flooded and she had a narrow escape when her horse plunged almost out of its depth. She found the town 'the dirtiest place I ever saw, not a bit of pitching in the streets its a perfect quagmire the whole City . . . though my chamber was near 20 steps up I had froggs and slow-worms and snails in my roome . . .'

Natural features that aided the traveller – such as a ford across a river or a pass through hills – gave a town a very strong advantage in the battle for survival. The traveller would obviously plan his route so that he could pass dryshod across a river, and the community that grew up around such a crossing would benefit from casual trade. The centre of gravity shifted from the Roman town of Great Casterton to Stamford (the 'stony ford' across the Welland) in response to this attraction. Guildford in Surrey had the double advantage of providing a ford across the Wey (the 'golden ford', rather charmingly named after the local profusion of marsh marigolds) and the entrance to a gap through the steep North Downs. Maidstone and Rochester stand at the southern and northern ends respectively of the great gap through the Downs made by the river Medway. Even the Romans were not averse to using natural features to facilitate town planning: Cambridge came into existence because it commanded a ford across the Cam.

Given the vital importance of the river, one may suppose that, in the absence of a ford, the building of a bridge would have been the first major communal activity, even though that bridge might have consisted of nothing more than stepping stones with slabs across like Tarr Steps in Somerset. Significantly, 'bridge-builder' is one of the proud titles of the Caesars – Pontifex maximus – a title so potent that the popes would gratefully inherit it and be known as Pontiffs. So important was the bridge in the life of the people that contributing to its maintenance became a recognized act of charity, a pious work that ranked with succouring the sick or visiting the imprisoned. In 1311, Richard de Kellaw, Bishop of Durham, granted 'forty days indulgence to all who will draw from the treasure that God has given them valuable and charitable aid towards the building and repair of Botyton bridge'. Gilds of religious laymen came into being with the express intention of preserving these links in human communication. The Gild of the Holy Cross in Birmingham

mainteigned and kept in good reparaciouns two greate stone bridges and divers foule and daungerous highways, the charge whereof the town hitsellfe ys not able to mainteign. The lack therefore wilbe a greate noysaunce to the kinges majesties subjectes and an vtter ruyne to the same towne, being one of the fayrest and most proffittuble townes to the kinges highnesse in all the shyre.

A curious office, that of road hermit, combining the role of warden, roadman and religious came into being. In 1458 the Bishop of Ely is appealing for funds for a certain William Grene:

Since our church at Ely is surrounded by waters and marshes and the relics of the Holy Virgin lying in it can only be visited over bridges and causeys requiring daily repair, we commend to your charity William Grene, hermit, who at our command has undertaken the repair of the causeys and bridges of Stuntneye and Some.

From bridge hermit to bridge chapel was a natural step. The splendid chapel to St Thomas of Canterbury which stood on London Bridge disappeared with that great structure but those at Wakefield and Bradford-on-Avon still survive, though that at Bradford-on-Avon was later converted into a lock-up. Both Wakefield's bridge and chapel excited the admiration of the sixteenth-century antiquarian John Leland: he describes them as 'a fair bridge of stone of nine arches under which runnith the river of Calder, and on the east side of this bridge is a right goodly chapel and two cantuarie priests founded in it'. These two chantry priests received £10 a year for their services through a foundation established in 1358 – the same year in which the chapel was built. Both bridge and chapel remained unchanged until traffic pressure in the nineteenth century made it necessary to widen it on its western side.

The rich man could gain much credit from his fellow-citizens by building a bridge. It is Leland again who describes how the bridge at Stratford-upon-Avon had become so dilapidated that people refused to use it and the town's trade was suffering accordingly. Thereupon a certain Sir Hugh of Clopton, a rich man who had been born at Clopton near Stratford and become Mayor of London, at his own expense built 'the great and sumptuous bridge upon Avon at the east ende of the towne, which hath fourteen great arches of stone, and a long causey made of stone, low walls on each side, at the west ende of the bridge'. A good bridge was a matter of great civic pride: Barnstaple boasts of having thrown a bridge over the 'great, huge, mighty, perylous and dreadful water named Taw'.

Houses appeared along bridges. The most complete pictorial record of this phenomenon is the series of sketches and paintings of Old London Bridge before the unofficial structures were banned in the eighteenth century. Picturesque they may look, but decidedly unsafe too, each building seeming to grope for a foothold, shouldering its neighbour aside. Lincoln's High Bridge survives intact, illustrating the changes and accretions over centuries. The vaulted arch is Norman, the houses that stand on the west side, making a continuous link with those on the same side of the street, are sixteenth-century. It, too, had a wayside chapel dedicated to St Thomas of Canterbury, but it was removed in 1763 and the obelisk which replaced it was in its turn taken down in 1938. The roadway is part of the modern pedestrian High Street. Publicity photographs are usually taken from water level on the east side when the bridge does indeed appear to be a well preserved gem. Less attractive is the appearance of the river itself, visually now little more than a ditch flanked by drab, mass-produced commercial buildings. Bath's Pulteney Bridge, on the other hand, is superb from whatever angle it is viewed. But that, perhaps, is to be expected of a work by Robert Adam in a city like Bath. Adam built it in 1770 – the only example of his work in Bath – and it is not a bridge but an exquisite building spanning a river.

Most town bridges remained little changed until well into the eighteenth century. Increased traffic led to the building of more bridges or, more often, a tinkering with existing bridges, strengthening them here, shoring them up there. Berwick-upon-Tweed has a remarkable series of bridges showing the changes in transport over some three centuries. The Old (or Berwick) Bridge, James Burrell, Surveyor to King James I between 1611 an consists of fifteen arches in a reddish sandstone. What it lacks in elegance it makes up for with a massive, confident dignity: from a certain angle the arches seem to be following each other across the Tweed like a herd of elephants. The New Bridge, built in 1928, is far more elegant to look at from river-level, crossing the river as it does in three swooping flights. Beyond these two – visible through their arches – is Robert Stephenson's majestic railway viaduct, the Royal Border Bridge, reminiscent of Rome in the way its great arches, powerful but graceful, rear up to carry the trackway on their shoulders.

The full difference between traditional and late twentieth-century technology is startlingly illustrated by comparing a modern road bridge over a river with any of its predecessors. Particularly instructive is the comparison between the beautiful bridge over the Thames at Richmond in Surrey, opened in 1777, and that of Chiswick a mile or so downstream, opened in 1933. The Richmond bridge seems to tiptoe out over the river so that the traveller is aware of being suspended in space. Yet simultaneously the bridge is an integral part of the banks on each side: the traveller is aware of progressing from one side of the river to another and that the bridge is a part of the living fabric of the town. The Chiswick bridge, by contrast, ignores river, town and banks. To the traveller standing in the middle of the roadway just before it launches itself out into space, the river is invisible. One is wholly unaware of being on a bridge: it seems part of the road system, shouldering its way forward, flattening everything around it.

A bridge intended to allow the passage of citizens could also only too obviously facilitate the passage of enemies. The fortified bridge was an equally obvious development. The bridge at Warkworth, in what was turbulent Border country in Northumbria, still possesses its defensive tower. Shrewsbury also had 'a mighty tower to prohibit enemies to enter onto the bridge' guarding the entrance to – significantly – the bridge known as Welsh Bridge. Chester, York and Durham all had bridge fortifications to inhibit passage on to them, but all fell victim to the demands of traffic, Warkworth Bridge surviving because the community it served never developed.

But even this quiet backwater had its problems. In the nineteenth century J. J. Jusserand recorded: 'Quite recently a gipsy's caravan was stopped at the tower on Warkworth Bridge being unable, owing to the lowness of the arch, to go under it. The pavement had to be hollowed out to allow the caravan to proceed on its journey.'

Until the advent of the canals made transport of cheap bulk materials even easier, towns were built for the most part out of local materials – literally being born of the soil. The more expensive town houses continued the use of local materials even into our own time. It is the flood of commercial buildings and the ocean of ordinary private houses that have employed non-local materials, blurring the identity of our towns. For if the town-plan is the skeleton and its history the spirit, the materials in which a town is built are its flesh, the means whereby it presents itself to the eye.

Traditionally, building materials fall into one of three or four main divisions, depending upon the nature of the soil and the crop it produces. Stone is the great building material in the north and west: timber and brick in the south: puddled earth and timber in the south-west: flint and brick in the east. But even within these broad divisions there are other divisions almost as broad. Haworth, in Yorkshire, and Chester are both stone-built towns. But Haworth is built of millstone grit, sombre in colour and almost as hard as granite in texture, resisting the frivolities of tournament so that towns built of this enduring but intractable material rely entirely upon proportions for their appearance. The red sandstone of Chester is not only easily workable but its warm colour gives an entirely different atmosphere to the town. Alternatively, different localities can use the same material in quite different ways. The plastered houses of Suffolk and Essex have turned themselves into a fantasia with pargetting – the delightful technique of decorating by raising the plaster in relief. It is such an obvious and easy way of giving personality to a building that it is curious that relatively few other areas using plaster – Surrey and Sussex in particular – have adopted it. Flint is used, too, both in its natural shape, and after being shaped or 'knapped'. It is one of the few naturally occurring materials still being used: flint workers refer to themselves as 'gathering' flints for use, rather than buying them, almost as if it were a species of wild crop. The difficulty of producing a flat surface from these irregularly shaped stones gave rise, in East Anglia, to the distinctive round towers of early Saxon churches, this being the means whereby their builders avoided the embarrassment of trying to make a corner. For their more important churches, the Saxons solved the problem by using flat stones for the corners. A later, sophisticated, development which produced an extraordinarily beautiful and durable surface, was achieved by squaring the flints. Two of the most outstanding examples of this are in Norwich – the black and white guildhall and a building erected as a mayor's house which later became the town Bridewell. A wall nearly eighty feet long and twenty-seven feet high is built entirely of cubes of black flint 'so admirably squared and so regularly put together as scarcely to admit the edge of a knife between the joints', as an anonymous historian, writing in 1832, noted, and his comments hold good today. The same writer quotes the remark of a contemporary architect:

The art of squaring flints in this curious manner is almost totally neglected, though I am convinced it might very soon be brought to perfection again by a little practice, from the facility I observed the workmen acquire, by a little practice, in repairing a tower belonging to the [bishop's] palace.

Timber was the most widely used material in the earlier centuries, a fact evidenced by the frequent and devastating fires that swept through town after town. It was usually used in conjunction with puddled clay or chalk or, later, brick but even here local uses varied greatly. In the north-west the wood itself was used as a medium of ornament, both in the famous black and white buildings of Cheshire, where the shapes of the beams themselves form patterns, and also where it was carved, as in that splendid example of high spirits, the Feathers Inn at Ludlow. In the east, the trend was to cover the timbers in a decent cladding: their builders would have been shocked by the current passion to expose everything that can be exposed.

Brick was a late-comer, even though the builders had the example of Roman buildings before them. Its use coincided with the opening up of trade with Holland, and the rising cost of wood as the forests disappeared, used up for building material and charcoal. Brick-making began again in the fourteenth century, got into its stride in the next hundred years and by the eighteenth century had penetrated into every town. But though the concept might be universal, the material would be local, so that every brick-built town has its identifying livery, ranging from lightest grey to deepest red and brown.

A major factor in the maintenance of homogeneity and identity was the re-use of materials. In the second half of the twentieth century the cost of labour is so high, the cost of machine-produced products relatively so cheap that it is far more economic to destroy materials and replace them with new than to preserve and use again. In the 1950s and 1960s the centres of most of our historic towns were perfumed for days on end with the smell of burning timbers, some of them centuries old. Until this century – until, indeed, the advent of the bulldozer – it was economically preferable to pay a man to conserve materials for re-use, rather than pay him to produce new material. Every town sited near an earlier major building that had fallen into disuse promptly cannibalized it as soon as the hand of authority was removed. One of the most remarkable examples of this is Castle Acre in Norfolk: the entire historic heart of the place is built out of the stone taken from the two vast flint-built structures, the castle and the abbey, which dominated it in earlier centuries. Many of the Roman bricks and tiles of Verulamium provided the building material for St Albans Abbey; the wall of the close of Salisbury Cathedral is built of stone taken from the cathedral of Old Sarum. The examples could be multiplied endlessly; the technique of re-use, introduced today as a bold innovation of conservation, was the norm in previous periods.

Conservation of energy was as important as conservation of material. Modern machinery enables the builder to dig down far below his predecessors' foundations to lay the foundation of his own towering building – a fact which poses grave problems for urban archaeologists. In previous periods, the builder would descend only so far as to clear loose detritus, content to lay his own structure over that of his predecessors. One of the results of this, as might be expected, was instability, and, indeed, the collapsing of major buildings – usually church or cathedral towers – was a commonplace in the mediaeval period. Such techniques lay up treasures for archaeologists. Excavations beneath the castle at Winchester uncovered a street which had built up an accumulation five feet deep, containing no less than eight successive road surfaces, in a little over 150 years.

One of the greatest of all urban influences, the castle, came in the wake of the Norman Conquest. Odericus Vitalis, the twelfth-century chronicler, was of the opinion that William would never have succeeded if the Saxons had possessed castles, for the invaders would simply have wasted their strength besieging strongpoints. As it was, the Normans swept through the land almost unopposed.

If the architectural achievement of the Romans was impressive, that of the Normans can only be described as astounding. The Romans were establishing themselves in a country whose inhabitants, though highly intelligent and courageous, were culturally their inferiors. The Normans were invading an established civilization whose inhabitants were culturally at least their equal. Neither was there a back-up system. If Aulus Plautius or Vespasian had been killed, there would have been no lack of generals to take over from them: if William the Norman had been killed at Hastings the course of history would have been changed.

The Norman genius for architecture was to have its full flowering in the twelfth century when the great cathedrals and improved castles began to soar up against a skyline that had known nothing higher than a church tower. But there is nothing to equal the sheer dynamism of those first few critical years immediately after Hastings when the small invading force set about subjugating a numerically superior, culturally equal, highly courageous and bitterly resentful population. And the major weapon they used was the castle. In five years they had erected thirty-three, most of them in towns, ruthlessly demolishing where necessary: in Lincoln 166 houses were pulled down to accommodate the castle, while in York it has been calculated that up to a seventh of the Saxon-Danish town was destroyed for the same purpose. By the time of William's death in 1087 there were eighty-six castles. Most were timber structures set on artificial mounds (although those at Colchester and London were built in stone from the first). The number of these mottes, or artificial mounds, was so great and their size so vast that many a historian was later misled into thinking that the Normans must have been utilizing mounds thrown up long before by Saxon engineers.

The work of turning hastily erected wooden palisades into permanent stone structures was the next stage, beginning a story of seemingly endless development, experiment, adaptation and change that would go on, for the individual castle, year after year, century after century.

The castle played an effective role in the town for an astonishingly long period. The fact that relatively few survive is an indication of that effectiveness. The sensible ruler, whether monarchical or parliamentarian, ensured that the castle he could not control, or which was redundant to his needs, was razed or slighted, in that splendid phrase which became popular during the Civil War. The length of time during which the castle played a military role was not only remarkable in itself – from the eleventh to the seventeenth century – but also in the changes of warfare that took place during that period. In the opening years the castle was defended, or assailed, by weapons and tactics that the Romans might have used; at the end of the period they were defeated, or assailed, by weapons and tactics that an artillery or tank commander in World War II might have adopted. They were erected, or demolished or altered, in response to changing social patterns around them. The anti-clericalism that went side by side with profound religious beliefs found expression in attacks on religious figures, in particular high prelates, who in turn defended themselves by erecting massive urban castles. In 1329 the Bishop of Lincoln turned his palace into a fortified defence. The Bishop of Wells followed suit in 1331 – creating a moated defence that is one of the outstanding charms of the little city today. The Abbot of Bury St Edmunds, after ferocious running battles with the citizens, erected the immensely powerful gate-house. Indeed, the unpopularity of the cloistered religious can be measured by the size and strength of these miniature castles, frequently all that remains of the abbey, as at Colchester and St Albans. The Bishop of Norwich turned his close into a walled city within a walled city.

Most surviving castles are to be found in country districts, where they have transformed themselves into that supremely English institution, the country house. But a few survive, as homes, in towns to give some idea of the social weight they pulled. At Alnwick, where the vast castle of the dukes of Northumberland is still a family home, a middle-class lady remarked: 'It's like living in a garrison town. Everybody in Alnwick works for the duke – and so everybody knows his or her place.' At Arundel the social life of the castle has an immense effect upon the town, the Duke of Norfolk and his family taking an active part in the town's affairs: the growing Arundel Festival owes much to that patronage. At Durham much of the castle was gutted to form the University in 1938, but enough of it remains to give an impression of life in the castle during the later centuries.

Long after the life of the castle had ceased, and the building itself been reduced to ruins, the effect of the enormous structure on a perhaps embryonic town would remain traceable for centuries. A motorist's frustration in the 1980s might well have been created by a military engineer in the 1080s, and a whole pattern of life might come into being in one place because of the presence of the castle in another. In Lincoln, the castle, and its titanic companion the cathedral, occupied most of the original Roman township on its high rock. As it happened, the Romans themselves had expanded the town, building a suburb down the steep hill and towards the river, and it was this area which became mediaeval Lincoln for all practical purposes, leaving the upper town to priests and soldiers. Today, in consequence, the upper town is left to priests, tourists and their ancillary services, with the lower town occupied by everyday industries.

Lincoln, with its population of 5000 or so at the time of the Conquest, was able to contain its castle without too much distortion but where the castle was tagged on to a small community, that community survived virtually as a parasite or client of the castle. Guildford had a population of perhaps 100 when the Conqueror's engineers raised their vast chalk mound and placed a shell-keep on top, and in consequence the early town shaped itself round the castle. At Ludlow the castle created the town. In 1066 a Walter de Lacy was granted the manor of Stanton and in return had the duty of holding the frontier against the Welsh. His son built that castle between 1086 and 1094, and a small market began to develop outside its gates. The town itself came into existence as a planned unit early in the following century, its role being to provide services for the castle as well as producing income for the lord of the manor.

Looking back at the era of the castle is to be impressed by the sheer beauty achieved by these grimly functional structures. The actual bones of most of the great buildings either have a sombre beauty born of strength, like Rochester Castle, or their builders actually introduced external ornament: the arcading on the west face of Norwich Castle keep is as beautiful as anything in the cathedral. And, by a quirk of history, in many a town the castle garden was the only piece of greenery the nineteenth-century citizens could enjoy and today it often forms the municipal gardeners' showpiece.

The castle was the symbol of the lord, of a despotism enlightened or otherwise. The town wall was the symbol of the citizens. The lord might well have had a hand in its beginning, but in its continuation and in its maintenance, spread over centuries, it was the work of the commonalty. Coventry did not even acquire its first murage grant until 1328, and the walls were not completed until 1539 – long after the mediaeval baron had followed the dinosaurs into extinction.

England's relative stability is well shown by the fact that there are no city walls to compare with the titans guarding Milan or Carcassonne or Florence. Nevertheless, although an Italian traveller envied the tranquillity of England 'with the sea as its wall and moat', well over a hundred towns in England and Wales were walled. When it is considered that some of the towns began building their walls only a few years before cannon, which ultimately spelt the doom of all walled towns, appeared in Europe – at Crécy in 1346 – it is evident that defence was only one reason for building a city wall, and perhaps not the reason foremost in the citizens' minds when they tackled the arduous, expensive task. Many sections were built on the cheap – ramshackle constructions on insecure foundations that obviously would never have withstood a determined assault. Some towns, too, began building their defences by constructing the gates: the first major construction on

York's great circuit was Bootham Bar, built in the eleventh century. In part, it is obviously necessary to defend a road ingress into the town, just as it was necessary to defend a bridge. But the role of walls and gates was as much economic as military: they allowed the citizens to control the comings and goings of 'foreigners' and levy tax upon their goods. Those foreigners might be peasants from down the road, or merchants from half-way across the world: the tax upon the goods they were bringing into the town, whether rolls of priceless silk or half a dozen eggs, contributed to the upkeep of the town. In a petition in Norman French, dated 1253, the 'foreigners' who lived just outside Norwich (*foyens du pays*) complained bitterly to the king when the citizens began walling the city: 'The strangers of the country who were wont to enter and go out of the said town at their will now cannot do so and the people of the said town of Norwich have disturbed their common ways.'

Following that basic principle of conservation of energy, the citizens as far as possible utilized the foundations provided by earlier engineers – perhaps centuries earlier. The mediaeval walls of Colchester, Chichester and Dorchester faithfully followed the Roman. At York, the engineers used the foundation of a Roman gate for Bootham Bar and the famous Multiangular Tower is pure Roman up to a height of nineteen feet. The mediaeval city of York expanded far beyond the Roman, however, occupying 260 acres (105 ha) as against 50 acres (20 ha). The earth ramparts were thrown up by the Danish kings of York, enlarged by the Normans and the stone walls upon them erected during the thirteenth century. Chester, too, expanded very considerably beyond its Roman boundaries, the engineers taking in the Roman walls where they coincided with current needs. The circuit of Chester's walls is entire, York's almost so – the former some two miles in total length, the latter nearly three miles. Their walkways are still in perfect condition – presenting indeed perhaps the easiest and certainly the most pleasant way of getting from one part of the city to another. Although not particularly high in themselves, their height relative to the town they defend gives the walker an extraordinary sensation of being in a low-flying aircraft, the vista changing imperceptibly with every step taken.

Like the castle, the walled city played an effective military role for a remarkably long period, despite the ominous and steady improvements in artillery. Elizabeth I, a penny-pinching monarch, thought it worthwhile to invest large sums to provide Berwick, 'the chief key to her realm', with the new-fangled Italian-style fortifications. During the battles of the Civil War they came into their own. Chester withstood intermittent siege for more than two years and was then subjected to heavy bombardments and assaults for five continuous months before surrendering to the Parliamentarians in February 1646. And there is a certain sense of historical fitness in the fact that Colchester, the first walled city of the land, should be the one to suffer the last great siege of England until, only after ten weeks of savage fighting, it surrendered to Parliamentary forces in August 1648.

In April 1942 the Luftwaffe launched what came to be described as the 'Baedeker raids' because they were specifically directed against the oldest, most historic cities of the land. They caused enormous damage to irreplaceable buildings, but unwittingly proved something of a boon for archaeologists, opening up much that had been hidden by building over the centuries. It came as a surprise to many cities to discover that they possessed substantial lengths of city wall. In most towns the gates disappeared towards the end of the eighteenth and beginning of the nineteenth century, falling victim to traffic pressure, but the walls had a very useful structural function: they could – and did – provide the back wall of many a house and commercial building, saving the builder at least one quarter of his expense.

In 1909 Norwich City Council instructed their engineer to make a survey of the city walls and report on their condition with a view to repairing them – a particularly enlightened approach for the period. The engineer's many photographs make clear what the tidying-up undertaken since World War II has eliminated – to what extent the walls were physically integrated into the post-mediaeval city. One remarkable photograph shows one section of the wall apparently sprouting chimneys – in fact, they are the chimneys of the cottages backed up against it.

Curiously, that pre-eminently twentieth-century phenomenon, motor traffic, has brought the city walls into prominence again. Many of the old walled cities, including Hereford, Canterbury,

Norwich and Colchester, have created an inner ring road, following the city walls, in order to ease traffic pressure. The speed and density of the traffic itself forms a moat, lapping round the walls that are again defending the vulnerable city within.

4

The Building of the Town

The pre-Conquest founding of towns was stimulated by war and religion: the post-Conquest by religion and trade, an elegant formula that encapsulates the development of civilization. During the twelfth and thirteenth centuries, at least 500 new towns were founded in a tremendous explosion of confidence and energy. As many again were developed out of existing villages while those that had been established before the Conquest received new form, new life. It is this period, above all, which brought into being the town as we know it today.

The Black Death put an effective end to that great burst of creation, but the stimulus had not quite died away even by the sixteenth century. In 1539 John Leland was admiring the new town of Bewdley:

The towne is sett on the side of a hill, so comely that a man cannot wish to see a towne better. It riseth from Severne bank upon the hill, by west, so that a man standing on the hill *trans pontem*, by east, may discern almost every house, and att rising of the sunne, the whole towne glittereth, being all of new building, as it were of gold.

Following his usual habit, Leland questioned the inhabitants regarding the origin of the place and came up with a theory to explain its spanking new appearance:

I gather that Bewdley is but a new towne, and that of old time there was but some poor hamlett and that upon the building of a bridge there, and resort of people to it, and commodity of the pleasant site, men began to inhabit there because that the plot of it seemed fayer to the lookers, took a French name Beaudley, quase Bellus Locus.

Leland was quite correct in assuming that the Bewdley he saw glittering in the sun was a new town that had been grafted on to a small village. Fifty years earlier the lord of the manor had established a series of weekly markets: their success generated the need for, and ultimate provision of, a bridge. This in turn drew in more people and in a little over a generation after the establishment of a market, the new town was flourishing.

It is not often that one has such a clear case of cause and effect presented by a knowledgeable eye-witness. Tracking down the physical origins of towns – that point in space and time when a chance collection of buildings becomes an urban nucleus – is a fascinating but ultimately irresolvable exercise in historic detection. The town may well have been in existence long before its first documentary reference. There was a mint coining money in Norwich at least a century before that reference in the *Anglo-Saxon Chronicle* telling of its destruction at the hands of the Danes. Those tiny, battered pieces of precious metal, bearing a crude picture of a monarch's head, are a priceless clue not only to the existence, but the status of a town. The coining of money would be kept very firmly under the monarch's control, and he would naturally choose an established – and well-defended – community in which to set up his mint. Like that of Norwich, the Guildford mint was turning out coins long before the town emerged into the light of recorded history when, in a brief codicil in his will, Alfred the Great bequeathed 'to Ethelwald, my brother's son, the manor at Godalming and at Gyldeford and at Steyning'.

Place-names help the enquirer to home in on the mother-site of the town. In Stratford-upon-Avon the parish church of Holy Trinity is in a district that has been known as Old Town since at least the thirteenth century. This would have been the village which was in existence when the Bishop of Worcester tacked on to it his own new town of Stratford. Conversely, the element 'new' in a place-name gives an obvious clue to the establishment of a new area: the streets named Newland in Sherborne and Banbury provide this pointer.

But somewhere the town itself should provide physical signs of genealogy. King's Lynn in Norfolk is an excellent example of a town that grew up in two main stages and left evidence of that growth, in two markets, each with its great church. The town lies on the shores of the Wash, a great inlet of the North Sea, much of which is uncovered at low tide. (It was during an incautious crossing at low tide that the ever-unfortunate King John lost his crown jewels.) A few traders established themselves at the narrowest point of the inlet, settling on land which belonged to the Bishop of Norwich. He built a small church here in 1101, and established a market beside it whose profits went to the Benedictine monks of Norwich Cathedral. The market took root and flourished splendidly, fed by the incoming trade that was to make the town a major seaport. Fifty years later the humble little church was replaced by a more splendid one (but so carelessly built on marshy foundations that the tower would collapse in 1453). Bishop's Lynn, as the town was called, was obviously prospering and the third Bishop of Norwich, in the 1160s, decided to establish another market. There was no room in the original borough, hemmed in as it was by two streams (the Purfleet and the Millfleet) and the king held the rights to the land adjacent. The bishop obtained permission to establish a market here, and built the chapel of St Nicholas beside it. The original market, controlled by the monks, was held on a Saturday and the whole complex thereby took the name Saturday Market, its young rival becoming the Tuesday Market. Operating separately, the two markets developed physically into totally different areas. Saturday Market is modest in size, an irregular triangle dominated by two superb flint buildings, the church of St Margaret and the Holy Trinity Guildhall. Tuesday Market developed into what has been called the finest 'built space' in the country, an immense irregular rectangle whose surrounding buildings, though erected at widely different periods, give the same impression of homogeneity – of being a vast, unroofed hall – as does Venice's Piazza San Marco. Eight centuries after the two communities were founded, eight centuries during which the whole urban trend has been that of unification, it is still possible in King's Lynn to be aware of passing from one locality to another – a sense of transition helped by the fact that the little Purfleet still stubbornly makes its way through the heart of the town, though its companion has been long since covered over.

Ludlow in Shropshire is another town which grew section by section, but here the unifying factor has been so powerful that it seems to be a single, homogeneous town. Salisbury, by contrast, was laid out much as a Roman town would have been by a single, autocratic will. The planner in this case was the Bishop of Salisbury himself. In 1220 Bishop Richard Poore, having decided that life was impossible on the hilltop of Old Sarum, established his cathedral by the river, then laid out the town to go with it. Influenced, perhaps, by memories of that cramped situation at Old Sarum with townsfolk, garrison and clergy all jostling together and bickering, he decided not only to make a really spacious ecclesiastical town within the town, but also to separate it as far as possible from the hurly-burly of the market. The result was the close of Salisbury Cathedral, the largest in England and one which, even in the twentieth century, seems to continue its founder's phobia, for it locks its gates at night, transforming itself into a little fortress. The market-place, producing valuable revenues but also the focus of red-necked unrest, was situated within the city ramparts but well away from the cathedral. The bishop kept his grasp upon its revenues until as late as 1795, when control passed to the city corporation, but the market is still separated from the cathedral and its close by the barriers of buildings. Unconsciously following the Romans, Bishop Poore laid out his city in the familiar grid pattern: to fly over the city at low altitude is to receive a deeply moving object-lesson in the power of human continuity, for Salisbury, in the 1980s, maintains the form envisaged by the bishop seven centuries ago. Originally the town had two main cross-routes running north-south, and two east-west: they have changed their names in places but still retain their direction. By the fifteenth century other streets were linked up in the grid, to produce the distinctive 'chequers' pattern, each square being known by a distinctive building within it – such as the Antelope Chequer, named after an inn.

Such an approach to town-planning requires the imprint of a master-mind and there are few other examples in England. Edward I founded Hull and Winchelsea, using that logical, sensible grid-pattern for these two towns which were to have such very different futures, and Abbot Baldwin created a similar scheme for the Suffolk town that would be known as Bury St Edmunds. Significantly, the best examples in Britain are the five little towns that Edward I set up as bastides or adjuncts to his five great castles in North Wales. Conwy, Caernarfon, Beaumaris, Harlech, and Criccieth were all laid out with wide straight streets crossing each other regularly and with a market-place at centre. The English town was left to create a rich tangle for itself – comforting to the citizen, enchanting for the tourist and infuriating for the traffic engineer.

Agriculture underpinned the towns. Even in the second half of the technological twentieth century, and even in that belt of densely populated country in the south-east known, pejoratively, as 'commuter country', rural life impinges upon urban. Dairy farm and suburban avenue lie side by side, tongues of agricultural land project to within a few hundred yards of many a high street. Until recently, the cattle-markets survived throughout the country in the towns that had given them birth, their sights and sounds and smells providing a link with a deep-rooted past. The tyranny of road transport has caused them to be banished to the outskirts – though here and there a few towns stubbornly cling to their traditional sites for the market. Ludlow is one such: each year some 8000 head of cattle and 25,000 sheep are brought into the heart of the little town, one of the factors that make Ludlow a truly three-dimensional town.

Farnham in Surrey provides a vivid picture of the relationship between agricultural prosperity and architectural beauty. When Daniel Defoe visited the town during his marathon ride round Britain in the 1720s, he discovered that the tiny town was

without exception, the greatest Cornmarket in England. So vast a quantity is brought every market-day to this market that a Gentleman told me he once counted on a Market Day Eleven Hundred Teams of Horse all drawing Wagons or Carts, loaden with Wheat at this Market every Team of which is supposed to bring what they call a lord, that is to say Forty Bushell of Wheat to Market; which is in the whole Four and Forty Thousand Bushell.

Defoe was, in fact, witnessing a relatively short-lived local boom. As late as 1620 Farnham's principal industry had been clothing manufacture. Then, in 1670, John Aubrey counted 400 wagons of wheat entering Farnham market, a long way short of Defoe's total of 1100 wagons fifty years later but still an impressive total for a little town in a locality devoted mainly to hops and sheep. Thereafter the trade in corn escalated, achieving a peak in 1694, according to the bailiffs' receipts. The reason was simple: a century of almost continuous continental warfare had prevented the wheat farmers of the south from sending their harvest north by the normal – that is, the cheapest – route, by sea. They had no choice but to send it overland, via Farnham. By the time Defoe was in Farnham things were returning to normal and trade was switching away from the town – when Defoe was in Chichester in the same year he noticed that

some moneyed men of Chichester have joined their stocks together, built large granaries near the Crook where the Vessells come up and here they buy and lay up all the corn which the country on that side can spare. They grind and dress the corn and send it to London in the Meal about by Long Sea, as they call it, now the War is over.

By the 1750s the corn trade in Farnham was declining but during the half-century or so that the little town had reaped the benefit of the abnormal situation it burst out into the Georgian splendour which now characterizes it. Apart from that architecture, the only traces of the great market now remaining are the pretty little yards with their entrances high enough to allow the passage of laden wagons.

Rus in urbe was the dominant characteristic of the English country town until the Industrial Revolution, hungry for space for its machines and workers, began to move in on the green fields within the town boundaries. Town plans before the eighteenth century show that as much as half the urban area was composed of gardens and orchards. Warren's map of Bury St Edmunds in 1748 and Godson's map of Winchester in 1750 show contiguous development only in the actual centre – along the High Street, in the case of Winchester, and in and around Abbot Baldwin's 'grid' in Bury, and even here the houses are liberally supplied with gardens. As late as 1807 Cole's plan of Norwich shows that at least a quarter even of this regional metropolis is open land. It is, perhaps, this memory of fields within the town boundaries which produced that ambivalent, contradictory but, to the English, meaningful term 'country town'. Long after the towns had achieved urban identity, the links with the great green sea that surrounded them remained. In Shrewsbury, the taxation of 1313 showed that most townsfolk owned livestock – one citizen had ten sheep. In 1354, pigs were such a menace in Norwich – 'divers persons have been hurt by boars, children killed and eaten and others [when] buried, exhumed' – that strict regulations for their enclosure were enacted, but even so the city council was obliged to allow pigs to roam free every Saturday afternoon in order to allow the styes to be cleaned. In Warwick, husbandry was the main occupation even under the Tudors, and as late as 1653 Newcastle upon Tyne had four assistant neatherds who every morning blew horns to tell the townsfolk to drive their cattle to the Town Moor.

And if agriculture underpinned the town, the market-place was the catalyst that transmuted otherwise random elements into the 'town'. A good working definition of the word 'town' would indeed be 'a place where people exchanged goods'. The market-place often developed more or less spontaneously at a cross-roads or outside a castle. The town plan of Alnwick in Northumberland shows this clearly enough: three roads crossed under the frowning protection of the great castle and, using these roads like the main strands of a web, over the centuries the citizens wove their town. Ludlow had a similar, but more deliberate cause: the town sprang up not over and around the cross-roads but as a market-place immediately outside the castle. At Stamford, the market-place developed outside the *burh*, in due course creating its own centre of gravity round which quite a new town centre developed. Other towns developed primarily with trade in mind, stringing themselves along a road to pick up passing trade: in due course that road would become the high street and the town would not trouble to create for itself a separate market-place. Guildford, Chipping Campden and Thame are three out of many which adopted this easy-going approach. Until the road-widening obsession of our own day blurred the distinction between country and town roads, the town plans of such 'linear towns' would show a characteristic cigar-shaped swelling where the ambling country road became the purposeful high-street-cum-market. At Chipping Sodbury and Montacute, a sudden sharp bend in the high road entering the town shows that it was deliberately re-orientated in order to pass through the market-place and so bring in customers willy-nilly. The Bishop of Lincoln diverted the Oxford-Aylesbury road in order that travellers would be obliged to pass through his newly established market town of Thame, adding a mile to their journey.

The Church was one of the great founders of market towns, creating on the lands it had acquired machinery which would generate wealth for centuries to come. Monasteries, which traditionally established themselves in virgin areas, were powerful instruments for such creations: they were also to prove remarkably tenacious – not to say tyrannous – overlords, grimly holding on to their rights even at the cost of pitched battles with the townsfolk (see page 102). The earliest of the few English planned towns, that of Bury St Edmunds, owes its existence to a remarkable Frenchman, Baldwin, Abbot of St Edmundsbury, who not only planned the titanic abbey but laid out the town to serve it immediately after the Norman Conquest. The vast scale upon which the abbey was built is well illustrated by the fact that two of Bury's great town churches of today – that of St Margaret's and the cathedral – appear as little more than chapels tucked into the grounds.

Abbot Baldwin planned on that logical, continental system of the grid. Immediately outside the main gate of the abbey was the market-place, an immense square – Angel Hill – which today challenges King's Lynn's Tuesday Market as being the most perfect built space in England, though its dignity is sadly marred by the cars endlessly parked there. In a very Latin, but decidedly unEnglish manner, Baldwin planned a great ceremonial avenue – today's Churchgate Street – which ran on an exact east-west axis from the town's West Gate, into the market-place and on through the great west door of the abbey up to the shrine of St Edmund. The destruction of the abbey church, and in-filling on the south side of the market-place has blurred the impact of the road's arrival at the abbey. Nevertheless, Churchgate Street still forms the major axis of the historic centre of Bury St Edmund's.

That encroachment on the southern side of Bury's great market-place is a common occurrence. One may confidently assume that the moment a market-place was established, traders and officials embarked on a tussle over encroachment which would continue over centuries. Even in the 1950s the Norwich Society took out an injunction against Norwich City Council to prevent the erection of permanent bases for stalls in the ancient market-place of Tomb-land, rightly believing that even in the twentieth century this could well be the thin end of the wedge. The Society was granted the injunction, the permanent constructions were cleared away and Tombland reverted to the appearance it had maintained for nine centuries. In a brilliant piece of detection the Ludlow Historical Research Group showed how one of Ludlow's most distinctive structures, the ancient building known as The Corner Shop, developed out of encroachments into the market-place that were never checked. From the point of view of the traders, dismantling and erecting stalls was a waste of time; from the point of view of the owner of the market rights, permanent stalls took up more space and diminished his revenues. Sometimes the lord of the manor, who owned the market rights, infringed the rights of the king who wanted to keep the highway open. At Thame, it was the bishop himself who was at fault: in 1221 he was accused of creating 'on the king's highway in the forum of Thame an encroachment where he raised houses to increase his rent, to the length of 100 feet in all'. At Wantage, in 1284, stalls were ordered to be demolished because they were narrowing the market-place so much that carts could not pass – but the following year the stalls were up again. In town after town evidence can be seen of the losing battle. Today they are charming little alley-ways that seem to start and stop for no discernible reason – like those in Ludlow – or isolated buildings, as in Eynsham. In Winchester, many of the streets that enter the High Street narrow at the end nearest the market, the now permanent result of stall-holders jostling for position just off the market-place.

The increased value of a site on or near the market is precisely measured by a royal edict at Scarborough: 'They shall pay me yearly, for each house in Scarborough whose gable is turned towards the street four pence, and for those whose sides are turned towards the street, six pence.' In other words, the citizen would pay less if the narrow end of his house fronted the market-place and therefore took less space. In the age-old game of dodging the tax-officer, some astute citizens created the L-shaped house, whose gable-end was indeed on the street but whose bulk was out of the taxable area. Another tax-officer's gambit was to levy tax on houses whose doors opened on to the square or market area: the citizen's response was to shift his door to a side alley. The public house currently known as the Studley Royal in Ripon market-place is one of many inns which adopted such a device.

One of the most beautiful and certainly most characteristic elements of market-place 'furniture' is the so-called market cross. In its oldest form it is simply a cross on a modest platform as at Winchester, Alnwick and Grantham: in its final developed form it can be an exquisite piece of architecture, like Chichester's or Malmesbury's. William Cobbett was particularly taken with Malmesbury's when he rode through the town on one of his rural rides in 1826:

There is a market cross in this town, the sight of which is worth a journey of hundreds of miles. Time, with his scythe, and 'enlightened Protestant piety' with its pick-axe and crow-bars have done much to efface the beauties of this monument of ancient skill and taste, and proof of ancient wealth; but in spite of all their destructive efforts this cross still remains a most beautiful thing though possibly, and even probably, nearly or quite a thousand years old. There is a market cross lately erected at Devizes and intended to imitate the ancient ones. Compare that with this and then you have, pretty fairly, a view of the difference between us and our forefathers of the 'dark ages'.

Until the thirteenth century, markets were quite commonly held in churchyards – a useful open space at the centre of the town where people congregated. In 1285 Edward I promulgated a statute declaring 'Henceforward neither fairs nor markets be kept in churchyards for the honour of the church'. No one lightly disregarded an edict of Edward I and the traders obediently moved out. But they had also become accustomed to meeting under the churchyard cross (bargains struck beneath it were regarded as particularly binding) and, in effect, they took the cross with them into the street: significantly, the earliest of the market crosses date from the early fourteenth century. Gradually the cross developed into a small, usually circular or octagonal building with seats round the base and a roof projecting from the pillar to provide a shelter for those who could not afford stall-holders' fees. Two centuries before Cobbett, John Leland described Malmesbury Cross as 'a right fair and costlie piece of work, made all of stone and curiously vaulted for poor market folk to stand dry when rain cometh'. Chichester's cross is, if possible, even more splendid. Bishop Edward Story gave this to his titular town in 1501 'to serve as a free market', setting it down firmly at the cross-roads where the two main Roman roads of the city met. Nearly five centuries later it is still at a cross-roads, a grievous trial and temptation to generations of traffic engineers and an almost miraculous survival in a period when motor transport takes precedence over almost everything else. Glastonbury's cross fell victim to traffic as long ago as 1803 but it evidently played an important role in nineteenth-century society for it was rebuilt in 1846. Salisbury had four beautiful fourteenth-century crosses, each devoted to different market produce, but only Lord Montacute's Poultry Cross of 1330 survives. Banbury Cross, immortalized in the nursery rhyme, was probably never a market cross as such but owes its fame to the legend of the lady from nearby Broughton Castle who had to walk three times round it at midnight to save her lover.

Gradually the crosses lost their religious significance as they changed their form. The lower storey remained open and continued to be in use as a small market area, but the roof-space evolved into an upper chamber. Ludlow's Butter Cross, built by a local architect called William Baker in 1743, is a complete classical building whose upper floor was used first as a town hall, then as a charity school. This use of the upper floor as a town debating chamber was widespread: the upper room of Wymondham's extraordinary cross, raised high on its spindly wooden legs, was used as a courthouse to try transgressors against market regulations. The upper storey of Bury's cross became a theatre in the eighteenth century.

Wymondham's cross is unusual in that it has been the subject of intensive research by a local history society who published an account of it in 1979. The author of the report, J. H. Wilson, traces the evolution of the cross from the late thirteenth century when it was probably a simple shafted cross standing on steps. Thomas Walsingham, the Prior of Wymondham Abbey, recorded in 1389 that a number of miracles took place by or near a cross standing in the public highway, almost certainly the forerunner of the market cross. This had become the usual elaborate covered cross by the sixteenth century, but was accidentally burnt down in 1615. Legally, the restoration of the cross was the responsibility of the lord of the manor – Sir Henry Hobart – but the citizens initially rebuilt it at their own expense, work being completed by 1618. Immediately afterwards there was a first-class row between the market traders and Hobart's officers who had begun to build shops in the market-place, a clear-cut example of encroachment. The citizens protested that the shops would leave 'no standing for cattell, nor convenyent place for people to walke in'. They complained further that they had 'built a fayer crosse, the rather to manifeste ther true & humble respect of your Lordship according to your request, which hath benn very chargeable unto them', implying that it was unjust that his lordship's men should seek to divert trade. Hobart responded in their favour, ordering work to cease upon the shops. The cross played a lively part in the life of the little town. Sermons were naturally preached from it, laws proclaimed and banns of marriage published from the steps: 'During funerals the corpse on its way to the Abbey Church was set down at the cross that those attending might pray for the soul of the deceased. Hence the term, "weeping cross".' Labourers and domestic servants congregated there for the Michaelmas hiring fairs.

A natural development of the market cross is the covered market or market hall. Undoubtedly the most famous, as well as the most beautiful, of all English covered markets are Chester's Rows. The first historic reference to the Rows as units occurs in the fourteenth century but there are a considerable number of earlier references to the *seldae* or stalls which were the predecessors of the present shops at street level. Whether or not the Rows are ultimately Roman in origin, there is some architectural evidence that this style of building was widely adopted, within the Roman city limits, in the late thirteenth century, perhaps as a result of the great fire of 1278 when most of Chester was destroyed. Today, they offer a unique urban experience, separating the pedestrian from the hurly-burly of the street while yet involving him in the life of the town, presenting an ever-changing vista as he moves along. For although each of the Rows forms a single unit, its individual components are delightfully distinct, each with its particular design of iron or wooden railings, some facing the street as an open verandah, others half-hidden behind massive arches, pillars and balustrades. It is an interesting commentary on the practical value of tradition that Chester's new shopping precinct, built just behind the Rows in Eastgate Street in the 1970s, is both efficient and attractive. In other towns, the so-called 'shopping centre' is only too often a brutally-designed, claustrophobic ziggurat dumped down into a town centre without reference to its host's topography. The Chester precinct is skilfully integrated into a mature area, its small central square actually inviting the pedestrian to linger while sheltering him from inclement weather.

The Butterwalk at Totnes perhaps lacks the charm and variety of Chester's Rows, but it, too, presents that highly civilized choice of a covered shopping area – a development one would have expected in all towns in so unstable a climate as England's. Those that were evolved in English towns have largely fallen victim to the shopkeeper's desire to bring his wares into the public eye, and the municipality's desire to have a tidy street front and a wider street to allow more traffic to move faster. Totnes's 'piazzas', as the parts of the arcaded street are known, are the most extensive survival in England though Ludlow, Winchester and Marlborough all have examples of houses projecting over the pavement area on pillars. The term 'piazza' is itself a misunderstanding of the Italian urban feature. Visitors to Bologna and Padua – and, above all, to the great Piazza San Marco in Venice – brought back with them a vague, confused memory of cool, colonnaded walks surrounding some great square baking in the sun, and applied the word 'piazza' not to the square but to the colonnade. The oldest building with this feature in Totnes is the house now known as the Pillar House in Fore Street: built in 1584 it cost its owner, Luke Seyrett, fourpence a year in tax because of the encroachment over the street. Gradually other citizens followed suit but the fashion did not become widespread until the eighteenth century, presumably after Inigo Jones's successful piazza at Covent Garden had set off a fashion. Unlike the earlier pillared houses, the arcades of the Butterwalk were built specifically to provide shelter for the stall-holders. As late as 1880 a local historian, P. F. S. Amery, noted:

'Until very recently the piazzas were occupied by the stalls of various traders whose right to their "standing" was independent of the owner of the house before which it was situated.'

The market hall and the arcade are variants of the same impulse – to protect the trader and the shopper from the elements – but the market hall is a direct descendant of the market cross whereas the arcade was a self-conscious, sophisticated device to tempt the affluent Victorian and Edwardian shopper. Chipping Campden's market hall is an excellent example of the former. Built by a wealthy local man, Sir Baptist Hicks, in 1627, it is a detached, arcaded building in the handsome Cotswold stone that gives the town its air of distinction. Like most such buildings, it is intended for dairy and allied produce (the term, 'butter market' is almost a synonym for these small enclosed markets). In Norwich, 'the Arcade' is a somewhat incongruous alley-way of glazed tiles and plate glass that was the Edwardian contribution to the market-place: pure kitsch though it is, it has through sheer length of life achieved a certain period charm which may guarantee its survival.

The corn exchange arrived in the early nineteenth century to contribute its distinguished façade to the market scene. Cobbett, that eminently practical farmer, was dead against it. Describing the corn market in Devizes he remarks:

The corn is brought in the market and pitched before it is sold and when sold it is paid for on the nail and all is over and the farmers and millers go home by daylight. Almost everywhere else the corn is sold by samples: it is sold by juggling in a corner: the mass of the people do not know what the price is and all this favours that monopoly which makes the corn exchange hands many times, perhaps, before it reaches the mouth, leaving a profit in each hand.

Whatever the social strictures that may be laid against them, the buildings themselves are usually remarkably handsome, usually doubling with some other purpose. The Guildford corn exchange, built in 1818 by public subscription, also served as the Assize Court. Salisbury's Market House, built in 1854, combined a remarkable number of functions in an equally remarkable looking building. The *Salisbury Journal* proudly described it as being 'in form an ancient Roman basilica', and its interior made lavish use of glass and ironwork, in a style apparently modelled on the Crystal Palace. It was designed to function not only as a corn exchange, but also as a corn store, a general market for vegetables, a cheese market – and a railhead. Local authorities seem to have taken a particular dislike to corn exchanges – presumably because they are not obviously quaint and antique in appearance – and scores have been ruthlessly demolished. Even two such handsome buildings as those at Guildford and Bury St Edmunds were once under sentence of death, Guildford's in 1935 to facilitate traffic movement and Bury's as late as 1958. But in the former case the town's traditional procrastination allowed the exchange to survive into a period when it was prized for its antiquarian value, and in the latter case indignant and popular reaction forced the local authority to rescind the demolition order. It was well restored (during which some fascinating bas-reliefs on architectural subjects were uncovered) and is currently enjoying a highly successful life not only as public rooms but also, ironically, as a corn exchange – one of the four largest in the country. In 1974 all but the façade of Salisbury's Market House was demolished, the site being used as a public library.

'The market' is the single strongest, uncontaminated link between the twentieth-century town and the town at any other period of its perhaps millennium-long past. Virtually every town has its market, and we have therefore grown accustomed to, and take for granted, this vibrant, untidy, colourful efflorescence which regularly brings life and colour to the town centre. It is a curious experience to enter, say, King's Lynn's Tuesday Market-place on a Monday evening, to walk in the great silent space where the heavens themselves form a roof, and then to enter it on a Tuesday morning when it has exploded into life. Where the lord of the manor used to battle fiercely to retain his lucrative market rights, his successor the local authority at best simply tolerates the market. Most would prefer to banish it to the outskirts, along with the odorous cattle-market but that vast, intangible but very real force, the popular will, insists on retaining this most ancient link with the past despite its untidiness and, in municipal eyes, its waste of space.

The so-called burgage plot – the land stretching back from the

street upon which the citizen built his house and had his garden –
is astonishingly tenacious as any property deed will show. The
façades of the buildings – and indeed the buildings themselves –
may well be eighteenth-, nineteenth- or even twentieth-century –
but a glance at a large-scale Ordnance Survey map of the street
will show that the houses are set on a mosaic of properties. The
value – and price – of having part of one's house facing the street
is reflected in the shape of the plots – long, narrow rectangles
which may well be divided and subdivided over the centuries or,
alternatively, combined to make larger properties but still manage
to retain their basic shape.

On 22 November 1263 there took place a macabre crime in
Norwich which, as by-product, provides us with one of the oldest
– though tantalizingly oblique – descriptions of a town house.
Eight men broke into the house of a certain Katherine, widow of
Stephen Justice 'doing great damage and robbery and burning the
body of her husband which at the time lay dead on a bier'. In the
subsequent trial, the physical description of the house played an
important part and from it William Hudson, one of the editors of
the city's Records, deduced the following:

The house stood around the courtyard into which would open all the
doors, and probably the windows, of the various apartments, the principal
of which was the hall, where meals were taken and visitors received and
here also the male portion of the household slept at night. To the south,
and entered from the hall, was the private chamber where the more
valuable possessions were kept ... Cooking was probably performed in
the courtyard, at least in summer and the site next the street was
most likely occupied by the store-room for the stock in trade or the
workshop ...

Evidently, Stephen Justice had been a substantial merchant. But
what were the houses of his poorer neighbours like?

Until recently, architectural history, like general history, focused
myopically upon the large, the important, the unusual. There will
be endless, detailed monographs on the church, the manor house,
the castle, the palace, but little or nothing on the buildings which
formed the homes of the greater part of the population. But with
improvement in archaeological techniques, and a shift in interest

towards social history, a picture is beginning to emerge of the development of the urban fabrics as a whole, and not simply that of a number of set pieces.

In 1979 a local history society, the Ludlow Historical Research Group, published a remarkable paper which traced the development of one street in Ludlow over some eight centuries. The street is Broad Street, and praises of its architectural beauties have been heaped upon it by writers from Leland to Pevsner. Visually, it is closed at either end – on the high ground towards the town centre by the eighteenth-century Butter Cross and on the low ground towards the river by the massive town gate called Broad Gate. Superficially, it is eighteenth-century in appearance – even the thirteenth-century Broad Gate is largely masked by an eighteenth-century building perkily developing from it but, as the Research Group showed convincingly, the street is the result of almost organic growth from the thirteenth to the twentieth centuries. One house, no. 32, displays this almost in textbook form: its foundations are of the early fifteenth century, the street front is late eighteenth-century – but the rear is sixteenth-century with an addition made in 1969.

In order to uncover the history of the street, the Research Group used a multi-disciplinary approach. Its members based their findings not only upon the rich collection of deeds and corporation minutes relating to the properties, but also upon the work of artists and photographers who over the decades have again and again recorded what Pevsner called 'one of the most memorable streets in England'. And, above all, they used the evidence of their own eyes. Clambering into lofts (the one area in a house least likely to be changed), poking into back gardens, measuring, comparing photographs with engravings and engravings with plans, the devoted members of the Group produced a three-dimensional picture of the growth of an ordinary English street. Ordinary – except for its beauty.

What emerges from this study is a picture curiously similar to that conveyed in the first chapter of Wells's *The Time Machine* where the Time Traveller, himself static, watches as the buildings around him rise and fall, expand and contract, changing their forms over the centuries. The earliest documentary reference to

Broad Street is a rent roll of the powerful religious organization known as the Palmers' Guild. The roll is dated about 1270, but internal evidence makes it clear that some of the houses were at least a generation old by then. Until the Reformation the Guild, and a sister religious body known as St John's Hospital, owned about one-third of the street between them. A powerful local family, the Foxes, managed to grab most of the property of St John's in 1537, but the estate was split up and sold within the century. The property of the Guild was acquired by the corporation which, in 1461, had become the successor to the lord of the manor.

'Some of the many cellars in Broad Street occupy cavities dug in the Middle Ages, but above ground no traces of any purely domestic buildings that can be dated before 1400 have yet been found.' The materials of these earlier houses would have been relatively cheap, ephemeral – clay, wattle and daub and the like. Every house was timber-framed until about 1700. The carpenters of Ludlow were a highly skilled race, using their massive oak beams decoratively as well as constructively. Their eighteenth-century successors disapproved of this display of the skeleton of a building and hastened to clad them where possible in brick. Socially, the street has always been mixed but with a bias in favour of the professional classes, a bias growing from the mid-nineteenth century onwards. And in purely human terms, one of the most remarkable things to emerge from the study is the stability of the street's population. In 1270 there were about 300 people living there: in 1978 there were 214.

It is, in general, the wealthy merchant's house which has survived to give the characteristic appearance of our historic towns. Four of England's oldest stone houses are associated with Jews, either specifically by name or by tradition. In Lincoln The House of Aaron the Jew was built about 1170 by a historical figure, Aaron, who managed financial transactions throughout England. The other ancient stone house in Lincoln – no. 15 The Strait – was built about the same period but is known simply as 'The Jew's House'. Moyse's Hall, in Bury St Edmunds – a rather bleak flint-faced building – and the house now known as The Old Music House in Norwich are of the same period and tradition. By a happy chance, many of our smaller towns that could not afford a custom-built museum have usually used the most substantial historic merchant's house for the purpose, not only preserving it but allowing public access to a building that would otherwise be private. Moyse's Hall is such a museum. The pious preservation of some great man's home also achieves the same purpose. Shakespeare's Birthplace in Stratford-upon-Avon tells us far more about a merchant's house of the period than it does about William Shakespeare, playwright.

Suburban development is by no means a twentieth-century phenomenon. Speed's plan of Stamford in the seventeenth century clearly shows what we would today call ribbon development – houses lining the two main roads leaving the town. In Winchester at the same period, perhaps a third of the population lived beyond the walls. Monasteries, with their heavy demands for space and the protection they enjoyed as sacred buildings, tended to establish themselves outside the walls. In Lincoln and Canterbury in the twelfth century, suburban living was considered more fashionable than living in the city centre. But, in general, to live beyond the town limits, in the *sub-urbs*, was to be disadvantaged. In the earlier, unsettled period it was the suburban dweller whose house first went up in flames at the hands of marauders: as often as not, too, on threat of attack the garrison commander would order the demolition of the shanties that had grown up beyond the walls. The suburban dweller was excluded from the privileges that the citizen had wrested – or bought – from the lord of the manor. It was not until the population explosion of the nineteenth century, together with the development of a technological society that simultaneously made living in town centres unpleasant and pro-vided the means of escape from it, that the drift to the suburbs became a rout.

Thomas Hardy's description of Dorchester, under the guise of Casterbridge in about the mid-nineteenth century, would hold good for the majority of smaller towns of the time:

Casterbridge was deposited in a block upon a cornfield. There was no suburb in the modern sense, or transitional intermixture between town and down. It stood, with regard to the wide, fertile land adjoining, clean-cut and distinct like a chessboard on a green table-cloth. The farmer's boy could sit under his barley mow and pitch a stone into the office window of the town clerk; reapers at work among the sheaves nodded to acquaintances on the pavement corner; the red-robed judge, when he condemned a sheep-stealer, pronounced sentence to the tune of Baa that floated in at the window from the remainder of the flock browsing hard by; and at executions the waiting crowd stood in a meadow immediately before the drop, out of which the cows had been temporarily driven to give spectators room . . .

'Casterbridge' in 1846 was doubtless an odorous town ruled by a brutal code of law where the desperately poor lived in the shadow of the immoderately rich. But as a town it was still an organic whole, contained within the circuit of its walls, an identifiable unit that was greater than the sum of its parts. It would see more change, qualitatively, in the next hundred years than it had in the previous thousand.

It may not be widely appreciated that in England we have our own, national, Atlantis. On the low cliffs on the coast of Suffolk, about four miles south of Southwold, a solitary gravestone clings a few feet from the edge. The gravestone marks the last resting place of John Brinkley Easey who was buried there in 1826. The rest of the churchyard, together with the church and what was once a major East Anglian port is below the sea. According to legend, you can stand on the cliff and hear, on certain occasions, the bells of the drowned churches of Dunwich tolling beneath the waves.

Dunwich was born of the sea, grew rich and famous through the sea, died by the power of the sea. Sometime in the early seventh century it began life as a small village on the shifting coastline. For five centuries the sea worked in its favour, silting up the harbours of its neighbours and rivals, enlarging its own. At the time of Domesday it was one of England's twelve leading towns, possessed of its own mint, and it even became the seat of a bishopric while Norwich was still a mere *burh*. It possessed seven parish churches, a monastery and a powerful merchants' guild and, by the time of Edward I, was one of the main ports of southern England. Then the sea that had given began to take away. A tremendous storm of 1287 washed away part of the town and silted up the harbour entrance. The men of Dunwich, a tough breed, fought back, digging out a channel and throwing up sea walls. But the sea came back again, twice more: in 1328 the harbour was wholly ruined, the rich fishing industry destroyed and in 1740 the North Sea took the husk of what had been a bustling seaport back into its bosom. The last of the churches and one more town gate have been engulfed within living memory, leaving a few ruins, a couple of isolated houses – and the solitary grave of John Brinkley Easey.

Dunwich is the most dramatic example of fate deciding against the town-builder. As against the scores of abandoned villages that lie beneath the turf and ploughland, there are no abandoned towns. But there are a few which have, as it were, fossilized themselves or shrunk into villages, and most of these are along that shifting coast of south-east England. Winchelsea provides a classic example of urban hubris. This was one of England's rare planned towns, proudly planted by Edward I himself after old Winchelsea had been destroyed, like Dunwich, by the mothering sea. New Winchelsea survived long enough to become an important port, but by the time of Elizabeth I the harbour had silted up and only sixty houses were left standing. There were a few indications of its great days when Celia Fiennes saw it in 1697 '. . . there are great vaults which was the merchants' cellars and ware houses; there was some few brass and marble statues in the Church but much demolished as was the church'. Today, the town presents a remarkable spectacle as though part of a Roman town had somehow continued to survive: the grid plan is clear but there is nothing within the grid but fields and, tucked into one corner, the village that inherited.

Further up the coast, Rye presents the perfect picture of a town frozen in time. The citizens had virtually stopped trying to fight the sea that was choking the harbour with millions of tons of sand when Celia Fiennes rode up the coast: 'Men now apply to quite drane the marshes for corn and grass rather than endeavour to cleare the channell of the sand, which if it were done would be the best harbour for shipps as formerly was.' There was a half-hearted attempt to restore the harbour, as Defoe reported on his visit in 1722: 'There is now an Act of Parliament pass'd for the restoring this Port to its former State, when a Man of War of 70 guns might have safely gone in: but 'tis very doubtful whether it will be effectual in the main end or no, after so long a time.' Defoe's pessimism proved justified: the sea continued to creep away and Rye gradually transformed itself into the picture postcard tourist town. But its situation gives it life: at dusk and dawn the great plain that robbed it of its livelihood is subtly transformed back into a sea, giving an unforgettable impression of what this powerful little town must have looked like in its heyday, with its immensely solid towers and walls defying the French, though proving helpless against the older enemy.

Proximity to a powerful neighbour can stimulate a town – or condemn it to a withering away. In Wiltshire the town of Wilton flourished under the Saxon kings. It was a *burh*, a monastic seat and a royal residence: as late as the reign of Edward I it was reckoned among the thirty leading towns of the kingdom. Then in 1224 a bridge was built at the newly-sited town of Salisbury, draining off the trade that used to go to Wilton. The merchants fought back – literally – ambushing the traders on their way to Salisbury and forcing them to come to Wilton. These violent measures did nothing to arrest the course of nature. The town retained its heart – a mayor and corporation, two MPs and a large market so that, unlike Winchelsea, it declined rather than disintegrated. There was enough money about to give the town an elegant eighteenth-century façade.

A few towns rise, decline almost to extinction, then rise again according to national stimuli. Thetford in Norfolk was one of the four major towns in England before the Conquest – its Domesday population was perhaps 5000. It was the seat of a bishopric until Herbert de Losinga transferred his cathedral to Norwich in 1095. Thereafter it went into a slow, unspectacular, but steady decline. In 1801 its population was half what it had been in Domesday and even in 1949 it was only a little over 4000. In 1952 Sir William Savage noted: 'Thetford seems to have slowly slipped into obscurity by an inability to keep its place or rise to its opportunities.' Then the small town was designated as one of those destined to receive London's overspill; the population soared and a completely new town was grafted on to the old. Most of the newcomers like it but there is little contact between new and old. '*That's* not Thetford,' an inhabitant of 'old' Thetford said, nodding at the crisp new town on the other side of the A11. 'I don't know what you call it, but it's not Thetford.' In 400 years, perhaps, 'old' and 'new' might be simply place-names, like the suffix used to distinguish the original village of Stratford-upon-Avon. But here only time can tell.

5
The City of God

The supreme symbol of our towns and cities is not the guildhall or the castle, but the tower and spire of the town church or cathedral soaring into the air; not dwarfing the town but transcending it, drawing together its myriad parts into one tremendous statement. The miracle of Salisbury Cathedral, glittering like marble and visible long before the town comes into view; Boston Stump rearing above the Fenland like a land lighthouse; Ludlow's tower literally crowning the town on its sudden hill – these are what the traveller remembers when summoning up the town in mind. Until this century, the probability is that the house of God was the biggest single building in the town. But size is not the final criterion. Even when, today, the dull brutish masses of office blocks shoulder their way above the skyline, physically dwarfing the church tower, it is to the church tower that the eye is drawn, not to the abstract rectangles filled with concrete and glass.

The church physically reflects its community. Churches in villages tend to remain static decade by decade, century by century. It is to these one turns when seeking the oldest models. The churches in the towns – particularly in the prosperous towns – change with the changing life around them.

In 1817 Thomas Rickman, an architect, wrote a book turgidly entitled *An attempt to discriminate the styles of architecture in England from the Conquest to the Reformation*. Rickman identified – or thought he had identified – four major classes or types of architecture in England and labelled them Norman, Early English, Decorated and Perpendicular. It was, in fact, a sensible classification, a useful piece of shorthand for professionals when discussing their work. But, like the academic division of history into 'periods', what began as a useful working tool became a tyranny. Architectural historians and guidebook writers, faced with this bed of Procrustes, lopped and trimmed and snipped in an attempt to slot the church under discussion into one or other of the periods. Inevitably some periods were regarded as 'superior' to others. Any connoisseur of ecclesiastical architecture has learned to dread the ominous phrase 'restored, 1880' – or 1870, or 1890 – any date, in short, when Victorian confidence, backed up by Victorian wealth, was attacking the churches of England and ripping out 'debased' architectural forms in pursuit of the pure 'Gothic' which fashion decreed was the only form in which God should be worshipped. Amateurs joined enthusiastically in the game. The reports of the Society for the Protection of Ancient Buildings are filled with horror stories of the time. A church in Lincoln

was restored throughout in the most approved fashion, except that the very ancient Norman chancel arch was for a time spared. It remained not long, for the young ladies of the Parsonage could not bear to see it. They found it wholly out of keeping and frightfully disfiguring to the new work, and so it was taken down.

To the long list of hazards that faced ancient buildings was now to be added bored young ladies turning from painting on velvet to architectural criticism.

The nineteenth-century obsession with 'restoration' is neatly matched by the twentieth-century's obsession with 'preservation' – town planners condemning this or that 'addition', trying to strip back to some impossible ideal period. Future historians may well use this obsession with physical details to mark that point in time when churches ceased to be religious buildings and became civic ornaments. It is a commonplace that they were built partly for social, partly for didactic reasons – the 'poor man's Bible', the concrete illustration of God's plan for man. Those who could not read, or for whom the sermon was so much windy sound, could see in the stained glass window the hope of resurrection for the worn-out body, could contrast it with the threat of hell so graphically carved on roof boss or arch. With that primary purpose in mind, the custodians of the building altered it as seemed appropriate to their generation. Here a head of Christ, worn smooth by time and weather, was confidently recarved in the current fashion; there a column was removed so that a bishop could be provided with his tomb, from which he could throughout eternity monitor the doings of his flock, receiving their prayers to speed him on to bliss.

There are perhaps 20,000 ecclesiastical buildings in England and Wales, of which about half would have been built in the period known as the Middle Ages. In some cases, the foundations would have been the work of a rich and powerful man, the lord of the manor or his equivalent. At Lavenham the great 'wool church', built between 1480 and 1530, was jointly financed by John de Vere, the lord of the manor, and the Spryngs, a local family of clothiers who had made a fortune out of the wool boom, an interesting example of a transitional stage of funding. But elsewhere it was the parishioners themselves who paid for 'their' church. The people of Bodmin rebuilt their church between 1469 and 1471 at an overall cost of £268 17s 9½d, contributing both cash and kind to the fund, as well as labour. One old woman sold her 'crokke' (metal cauldron) and gave the money to the building fund; a 'hold woman' contributed 3s 2½d; the maidens in Fore Street and Bore Street gave subscriptions; the 'parish peple' who actually lived outside the town gave 19s and even the vicar contributed a year's salary.

In the mediaeval period both cathedrals and churches discharged the kind of social role that would today be discharged by civic and concert and market halls – indeed, by restaurants, schools and any form of building where people meet for social purposes. The people had themselves built their church and it was, in addition, probably the only large waterproof building in the town. In times of war, or social unrest, it provided a refuge. The citizens therefore were perfectly accustomed to using it for a variety of purposes which today would be regarded as sacrilegious. In 1358 Exeter Cathedral had to promulgate a ban on drinking parties in the building – the intention seems to have been to regulate, rather than prohibit. At St Audrey's Fair in Ely stalls were erected in the cathedral for selling ribbons and lace ('St Audrey's Lace' gives us the useful word 'tawdry'). The people of Salisbury went one better, actually using their cathedral for a horse market.

Pews were unknown in the early period. Even as late as the 1820s William Cobbett, that sturdy defender of the traditional, was inveighing against the use of pews in churches:

Those who built these noble buildings did not dream of disfiguring the inside with large and deep boxes made of deal boards. This lazy lolling in pews we owe to the Reformation. A place filled with benches and boxes looks like an eating or a drinking place, but certainly not a place of worship. A Frenchman went to church along with me one Sunday. He had never been in a Protestant place before. Upon looking round him and seeing everybody comfortably seated, while a couple of good stoves were keeping the place as warm as a slack oven, he exclaimed 'Pardi! On sert Dieu bien à son aise ici!' That is – 'Egad! They serve God very much at their ease here!'

The pews to which Cobbett would have been accustomed, albeit disapprovingly, were elaborate boxes that did indeed look like private dining stalls in an inn: the little church of Holy Trinity in York has a complete set of these box-pews which effectively prevented the traditional use of the floor area for social purposes.

Outside the church is the churchyard, God's Acre, the town cemetery until burials in the town centre ceased in the nineteenth century. The church would usually be built upon a pre-Christian site (it's a sobering thought that the green area next to the multi-storey car park or overshadowed by the new office block has been a sacred site for a thousand years and more) and in a large number of cases the burial ground would precede the church. But this sombre use did not preclude the area being used for mundane and indeed light-hearted purposes. In general, the north side of the churchyard would be used for non-secular purposes – for markets or for sports (archery and wrestling were particularly popular), leaving the south side for burials. Mediaeval grave-diggers were notoriously indifferent to the sites of earlier graves. The grave-digger in *Hamlet* casually picking up a skull is by no means unusual. Space was at a premium and a new corpse would be buried on top of an earlier one as soon as the course of nature made it possible. A chilling demonstration of the effect of this can be seen in the graveyard of St John Maddermarket in Norwich. The level of the ground is chest-high compared with the level of the road surrounding it. These packed graveyards, their occupants covered ritually rather than adequately with earth, would have contributed substantially to the 'plague' that periodically swept the towns.

In keeping with that casual disposal of the dead, there were few memorials to ordinary people before the eighteenth century. Those that appeared were, until the nineteenth century, governed by the nature of the local stone. In the north, the hard millstone grit and granite allowed only plain, massive headstones with the absolute minimum of ornament and lettering. The tendency here was to lay them flat and the grim effect they produced is well displayed by that awful churchyard in Haworth, whose proximity to the Brontë rectory added so much to the tragedy of those lives. The slate quarries of the Midlands produced headstones which allowed the mason almost the skills of a writing master. East Anglia and the south had little stone, and the headstones were mainly in wood, among them that dead-board or leaping board which bears such an unsettling resemblance to the headboard of a bed. In the late nineteenth century the satisfying relationship between local geology and the stones used for monuments was destroyed with the advent of commercially produced stone from distant quarries – white marble from Italy, pink granite from Aberdeen, lettered in showy gilt and garnished with acid-green chips, turning a sober, dignified resting place into a gaudy travesty. The current tendency is to banish all stones, removing the unsettling reminders of mortality, turning the churchyard into a 'municipal amenity'.

The difference between church and cathedral is one of function, not of form. The great abbey of St Albans, though at least 800 years old, did not become a cathedral until 1877. Southwell, too, although built in the early twelfth century, did not become the seat of a bishop until 1884. Conversely, the undistinguished late eighteenth-century parish church of Holy Trinity in Guildford was designated a cathedral when the new diocese of Guildford was created in 1922. It remained such until the new cathedral was consecrated in 1961, when it reverted to its status as a parish church. It is simply the presence of the bishop's throne, his *cathedra*, which determines the status of the building. And, contrary to popular opinion, the presence of a cathedral does not automatically make a community into a city. All cities have cathedrals, but not all cathedrals are in cities.

Nevertheless, popular opinion, though technically wrong, is emotionally right in assigning a different nature to a cathedral and to its host community. A cathedral does indeed 'feel' different from a church and a community that possesses a cathedral does indeed have a greater dignity than one that does not. It may be the cathedral's more impersonal nature that distinguishes it emotionally from the parish church: its memorials commemorate national figures, rather than the local butchers and haberdashers and corn chandlers who rest in and around the parish church. Its architectural alterations are on a grander, slower scale than those which have been inflicted upon its smaller sister. The peculiarly Anglican system of church preferment means that the parson is virtually pope within the confines of his parish, until this century free to do what he liked with the physical church that had fallen to his care. Changes in the cathedral had to go through the net of the dean and chapter, and in consequence the hand of the Victorian restorer has lain less heavily upon it. The cathedrals have not altogether escaped, however. In the late nineteenth century the Society for the Protection of Ancient Buildings carried on a running battle with the dean and chapter of Exeter Cathedral who were restoring the great West Front. 'The Dean and Chapter apparently argue that the more money expended the more virtue there is in the work,' the Society lamented, calculating that over £80,000 had been collected and spent on the deplorable activity. 'It would be less injurious to the building, and a less violent exercise of their power, if they were to cut their names in great letters across the front.'

One of the more nonsensical legends which developed out of the Gothic revival was the belief that the mediaeval masons built purely for the love of God, content with nothing more than their keep – and moreover building instinctively with nothing so mundane as architectural plans to guide them. Both concepts are pure romance. The mason was a highly skilled specialist who demanded, and received very good payment for his work. And while there was no architect in the sense that Wren was the architect of St Paul's, there was undoubtedly a master mason who would receive instructions from the authority funding the building, and co-ordinate the necessary army of workmen. Nevertheless, even while emphasizing the commonsense fact that the builders of the cathedral must have approached the task in a practical manner, it must equally be emphasized that these vast, unprecedented

Elm Hill, Norwich: a model of urban preservation

Norwich Cathedral, viewed across the Grammar School playing fields. The Watergate, through which building material was transported, is behind and to the left of the observer

The sheer mass of stone used in the building of the cathedrals could not be more clearly shown than in this view of the West Front of Lincoln Cathedral, taken from the ramparts of its neighbour, the Norman castle

The same viewpoint but taken from ground level looking towards the Exchequer Gate, one of the massive gates of the close. Both cathedral and castle are just within the circuit of the walls of the original Roman city

An unusual view of the back of High Bridge, Lincoln, showing how it has been physically integrated into its neighbours on one side of the stream

Steep Hill, Lincoln. The observer is looking down the hill, with his back to the cathedral: at the bottom of the hill is the later Roman extension of the city

Wisbech and Bewdley are among the few English towns which
continue to make a feature of the river which gave them birth

Bath – grey stone houses set in a green hollow

The Market Cross, Salisbury. This, the Poultry Cross, is the last survivor of Salisbury's four market crosses. It still provides shelter for traders on market day and for footsore tourists at all other times

The calm of the Established Church: Cheyne Court and the Priory of St Swithin's, Salisbury

A picturesque beauty spot now, the simple bridge of stones at Tarr Steps, Somerset, was once a vital crossing point – the archetypal bridge

One of many cottages at High Roding in Essex, where the art of pargetting has given great individuality to plastered walls

The embattled Church: at St Albans the Great Gateway of the abbey is also a fort

Part of Hereford's ancient city wall was uncovered during post-war developments

The Market-place, St Albans, with the town hall in the background. On the right is the tower of the abbey whose presence originally generated the market trade

HERE
Lye the Remains of
ELIZABETH GAY
Who after a Service of
Forty Years
finding her Strength diminished
with unparalleled disinterestedness
Requested that her Wages might
be proportionably lessened
She died July 7th 1789

As a testimony of their Gratitude,
for the Care she took of them
In their tender Years, this Stone
Is Erected by the Surviving Daughters of her late Master and Mistress
CHRISTOPHER and ELIZABETH WARRICK
of Park in this Parish

In St Clement's churchyard, Cornwall, lie traditional tombstones of local material

The guildhall at Lavenham in Suffolk had a particularly interesting history, having been used variously as a lock-up for the rector of Hadleigh before he was burnt at the stake, a town hall, a prison, workhouse, almshouses, a refuge for evacuees, a 'British restaurant' and a nursery school. It is now owned by the National Trust

Norwich guildhall, with the heraldic lion of the modern city hall in the foreground

The King's Head, Aylesbury, now owned by the National Trus
began life as a monastic hospice

An early photograph, dating from 1870 and taken from a glass negative, of the last cattle market to be held in central Guildford. Few of these precious glass plates survive today

Pride of ownership – the doorways of this otherwise
undistinguished row of 'two up and two down' in an Edwardian
suburb have these lively hand-carved lintels

projects argue an astonishing community and continuity of purpose. Their economic investment must have represented for the community the equivalent today of building a Saturn rocket, at the very least. It is as though present-day Exeter or Wells or Lincoln had each decided to design, construct and launch its own, civic, moon probe. The populations of the cities that built them were measured in the lower thousands. In some cases, the entire population of a city could stand in the cathedral it had built. Construction might go on over generations. England has nothing to compare with the cathedral at Milan whose building extended over six centuries, but a hundred years and more was a commonplace. Salisbury was one of the few whose erection took place during a single lifetime; Lichfield's occupied 125 years – and even that was the third upon the site; at Winchester the Normans demolished the Saxon minster (which had itself been rebuilt twice) to begin their own monster. The builders were advancing into unknown territory: apart, perhaps, from the temple of Claudius at Colchester, no building on this scale had ever been contemplated before. One can get some idea of the builder's reaction to the problem of size by comparing the squat solidity of the earlier Norman buildings with the grace and elegance of the later buildings as their builders gained confidence and experience, substituting balanced stresses for masses of stone. It has been calculated that one of the pillars at Durham Cathedral contains as much stone as half the nave pillars in Westminster Abbey. The extent to which the builders worked on an ad hoc basis can be shown by the fact that their successors had to improvise supports when the foundations proved inadequate. The beautiful inverted arches at Wells were built in 1338 to check the alarming settling of the central tower. At Salisbury in 1330 a tower and spire, weighing 6400 tons, were added without providing additional foundations. The great weight distorted the building, actually bending the supporting pillars, and transept arches were added to take the strain.

Where possible, the builders used local stone, opening up quarries specially for the purpose. The pale, distinctive stone of Salisbury Cathedral comes from Chilmark some ten miles away; Wells's is from Doulting, eight miles distant. Where stone had to be brought over long distances, water transport was vital. Cathedrals in

East Anglia presented a particular problem for either there was no local stone, as at Ely in the fenland, or the local stone was deemed not suitable – like the flint in Norfolk. Stone was therefore brought by waterway from the same quarries that supplied Stamford, while for Norwich, situated on a navigable river, it was easier and cheaper actually to fetch the stone from France. It was brought from Caen, across the Channel and up the Yare and, for the last few hundred yards of its journey, a canal was dug to the site. It was filled in afterwards, but the Watergate remains one of the city's most beautiful and distinctive buildings.

The architectural feature that undoubtedly distinguishes the cathedral not only from the parish church but also from its continental peers is the close, that pre-eminently English institution. Defoe's description of Salisbury Close (which was also the model for Trollope's Barchester) can fit most:

This society [of Salisbury] has a great Addition from the Close, that is to say the Circle of Ground wall'd in adjacent to the Cathedral in which the families of the Prebendaries and Commons, and others of the Clergy belonging to the Cathedral, have their Houses, as is usual in all Cities where there are Cathedral Churches. These are so considerable here, and the place so large, that it is, (as it is called in general) like another City.

The closes differ from each other as greatly as do their parent cathedrals yet, like the parents, they possess much in common. There is usually at least one massive gatehouse, and commonly two, whose upper storeys have had a variety of uses: St Ann's Gate in Salisbury was a music room where Handel gave his first concert in England. Somewhere is the choir school and, perhaps, the grammar school of the town. The houses, usually surrounding a central green, belong to virtually every period since the building of the cathedral. Salisbury's is particularly well documented. The oldest recorded occupancy is no. 15, known as Hemingsby House from its earlier occupant who died in 1334: it possesses what was evidently a chapel, as well as tiles from Old Sarum. Further along is the splendid seventeenth-century house known as Mompesson House from the Wiltshire family who built it in 1701. The family first established themselves in the close in 1635, acquired the leases of the houses on the site not occupied by Mompesson

House, demolished them and built their own mansion. Demolition is the exception rather than the rule, however, the houses in most closes surviving to show almost a textbook sequence of architecture. Skilfully, they adapted their roles to survive even the upheaval of the Reformation. In 1348 Bishop Ralph founded Vicars' Close in Wells, a range of forty-two cells in a college for deputies for the senior clergy: many were adapted after the Reformation to make married quarters.

The coveted leases are distributed very much on a grace and favour basis, with first choice being given to clergy and cathedral staff. In some of the closes a few commercial organizations have made a discreet appearance – lawyers and the like for the most part – and the majority (although certainly not all) have given up the beadles who used to police them. But they are still a world apart.

Most of our great cathedrals are approaching their millennium. Compared with the great monuments of the pre-Christian world – with Stonehenge and Avebury and even the ruins of Rome – they are still in their adolescence, but these older monuments are simply masses of stone, decaying at the same rate as the hills decay. The main mass of the cathedral may be of stone, but it is of a stone chased and pierced until it seems to be of filigree, a total contrast with the monoliths of the past. And within that frame are held organic or man-made materials – wood, metal, glass. Some of these materials are so old that they are changing their very structure. At Canterbury the stained glass resembles the cataracts of an ageing eye. 'The deterioration is far advanced and it will take all the resources of scientific skill and equipment to save it,' says a leaflet appealing for funds.

They have not been cosseted, these delicate titans. Again and again over the centuries they have been the targets of hatred and fanaticism. In England, the fury of Puritan iconoclasts followed the greed of Tudor depredators. John Evelyn records how, at Lincoln, a gang set to work on the brasses: 'They told us they went in with axes and hammers, and shut themselves in, till they had rent and torne of some barges full of mettal; not sparing the monuments of the dead, so hellish an avarice possessed them.' In Norfolk an itinerant iconoclast kept a careful record of the blasphemous windows he smashed in; in Wiltshire a cannier man was selling the glass of Salisbury Cathedral as late as the eighteenth century. He was after the lead, and the glass was of no use to him. And even after the cathedrals had ceased to be the object of active hatred, they suffered from their dominant role as the city personified, for in the heart of their cities they were subject to endless vibration as traffic increased, and their fabric was eaten away by chemicals poured out from chimneys and exhausts. World War II brought a new hazard – aerial bombardment – with the cathedrals themselves as prime targets in the so-called Baedeker raids.

Financially, the building and maintenance of the cathedral was one of the first charges on its parent community, yielding precedence only to defence. Today, ironically, as the cost of maintenance rises, income descends. The rich man today is far more likely to endow a university chair or a charity than to build a chapel or insert a window. The trade union, lineal descendant of the guild, ploughs back spare cash into pensions and future strike funds rather than donate it to the repair of a tottering building. Restoration appeals are now constant. In 1954, when Westminster Abbey appealed for £1 million, it hit the headlines. Today that sum is viewed virtually as a preliminary. Wells Cathedral appealed for £1,300,000 to restore the West Front; Canterbury asked for £3,500,000, much of it earmarked for the stained glass. Of all the problems of preservation that face us, the cathedral is dominant, raising the question – who will build the cathedrals of the future when these, at last, are gone?

A physical characteristic of most cathedrals is the cloister of the monastery into whose keeping it was confided when first built and nearby, in many a close, are the ruins of the monastery itself. Thirty-five towns were founded directly by, and for, a monastery but in addition some hundreds of towns were directly influenced by the presence in their midst of such a huge, wealthy, influential autonomous body. The high peak of monastic foundations was in the thirteenth century when there were about a thousand houses in England, the largest being that of St Albans with a community of over a thousand souls. Altogether, there were perhaps 20,000 religious of both sexes in a population of some three million. Allowing for some 40,000 servants and dependants one may calculate that in thirteenth-century England at least one person in fifty was living directly off the monastery.

Today, one of the strongest evocations of urban peace is the cathedral cloister and monastic ruin with shaven lawns, cooing doves, silence broken only by the chiming of the clock or sound of distant singing. But these same oases of peace were frequently the scene – indeed, the cause – of the bitterest fighting in urban history, the tussle between townsfolk and clergy. The abbot not only held extensive rights over the town which the monastery might have brought into being, but exercised those rights with a quite remarkable degree of tyranny. At Cirencester, the burgesses held their lands only on a life tenure: not only were they debarred from transmitting property to their children, but they were also obliged to pay a 'fine' to the abbot on a daughter's marriage and, at death, the abbot took their best chattel as a 'heriot' in his capacity of abbot, and their second-best chattel in his capacity of rector. At Bury St Edmunds the abbey controlled almost every part of the town's life, in particular the vital and lucrative business of buying and selling food. The abbey had the right of buying up (forestalling) food before it came on the open market and expected to pay ½d a hundred less for herrings. Tax was levied on the town fields and on flax, a major local crop, while the abbey had the odorous but very valuable monopoly of manure in the streets. A particularly irksome right, which both here and in other towns was the cause of endless friction, was the obligation laid upon townspeople to grind their corn at the abbot's mill. It presented the maximum irritation to the townsfolk for not only did they have to cart their corn across the town to the mill and pay for the privilege, but the abbey's miller cheated as a matter of course, returning less meal than the corn he had received. Again and again the abbey's bailiff would make the rounds of the town, seizing and breaking up illicit hand-mills. At St Albans, in a cynical display of power, the confiscated millstones were used to make a path in the abbey cloister and in one of the violent reactions against the monks, the townsfolk broke into the abbey and tore up the offending millstones. Usually the monarch took the part of the abbey but in Cirencester the citizens were able to obtain a charter from Henry IV, giving them a considerable amount of self-government and abolishing a wide range of taxes. The abbot bided his time, keeping account of all the rents and taxes due. Thirteen years later Henry V cancelled the charter and the abbot promptly presented the enormous bill of £6000 for arrears.

The citizens' resentment again and again took the form of open riot. In 1327 the people of Bury rose against their monastic overlord, killing several monks, burning part of the monastery and carrying off the abbot. He at least survived but during the Peasants' Revolt in 1381, when the abbey again became a focus of rebellion, the abbot was beheaded. At St Albans during the Revolt, the people broke into the abbey, released the prisoners from the abbey prison and burnt the deeds that specified their servile duties.

On the credit side, the abbeys and monasteries formed a species of economic reserve. It was they who created the wealth they later enjoyed and which attracted the hungry attention of Henry VIII. Friaries were usually established in the town itself, for the life of the friar, as opposed to that of the monk, was spent 'in the world' (hence the prevalence of numerous Blackfriars or Greyfriars Streets). Monasteries were commonly established on virgin land which, over the years, was turned into valuable farmland, creating wealth and attracting settlers. Their role as educationists, and as refuge for the poor and sick in a society which saw no particular reason to legislate on behalf of the weak, was also vital.

The end of the deeply-rooted, powerful and centuries-old system came with remarkable speed. The Act of Dissolution was passed in 1536, and by 1540 virtually all abbeys and monasteries had been suppressed. Most of the monks and nuns were either pensioned off or – where qualified as priests – slotted into the secular system. But the buildings and their contents became the object of one of the greatest acts of plunder in history. The king's friends acquired the great buildings for a song: the number of existing 'stately homes' whose name includes the title Priory or Abbey is significant. At Bury St Edmunds a certain John Pryer acquired the entire vast property for £412 19s 4d. The great palaces and churches, part of the nation's architectural heritage, survived or were destroyed on a random basis. The abbot's palace at Bury was used as a residential house until 1720 before disappearing, but the rest of the building immediately became a quarry for the townsfolk. At Tewkesbury, however, the citizens saved the superb abbey church after the rest of the abbey had been demolished by claiming that it had always been their parish church. The Crown sold it to them for £453.

The break-up of the monolithic Roman Catholic hegemony inevitably resulted in an increasing fragmentation with ever more, ever smaller sects claiming a place in the sun. The French gibe that the English have a hundred religions but only one sauce has a kernel of truth. But the religious fragmentation brought about an architectural bonus – the creation of Nonconformist places of worship.

Turning their backs upon the dogmas of the established and the Roman Churches, and rejecting their gorgeous ceremonials, Nonconformists – whether Quaker or Baptist, Congregationalist or Methodist – wanted a place of worship that would reflect their own plain faiths. The industrial towns and cities of the North were the breeding ground for Dissent, but the new places of worship sprang up in virtually every town in England. They appeared even in the villages. In East Anglia, for example, it is probably true even today that religious dynamism has moved from the splendid parish church to the gaunt little chapel. Among urban communities, however, though the chapels might be plain, they were anything but gaunt. In Norwich, under the very shadow of the great Norman cathedral rose the exquisite Wesleyan meeting house known simply, from its shape, as the Octagon Chapel. It was built in 1756 by the same Thomas Ivory who built the elegant Assembly Rooms (see page 126), and it excited even Wesley's admiration. 'How can it be thought that the old coarse gospel should find admission here?' was his remark on seeing the elegant building.

Norwich's Octagon Chapel was, admittedly, built at a time of architectural genius in a city with a splendid architectural tradition. But throughout the country, in the most unlikely places and at a time when British architecture was entering the doldrums, the Nonconformists were raising their little jewels. Unlike their co-religionists in the Established Church they felt no compulsion to clothe religious faith in an ever more debased 'gothic' but returned to an earlier form, the classical, relying for effect not on ornament but on line and proportion. Each is individual. The Unitarian chapels at Bury St Edmunds and Chesterfield in Derbyshire are quite different, the former emphasizing its brickwork and splendid arched windows, the latter coolly elegant with classical quoins and pediment. At Walsingham the Methodist chapel is virtually indistinguishable from a private house. Even in the second half of the twentieth century when architects of the Established Church have been set free, producing such examples as the cathedrals of Coventry and Liverpool, the new Nonconformist chapels in the smaller towns are frequently more interesting, more experimental, than their Anglican brethren.

Tucked in the shadow of many a parish church or cathedral is an offspring of the monastery that continues to flourish in the twentieth century – the almshouse. Every monastery had a *hospitium* where travellers and strangers were entertained overnight or treated to a meal on their journey. The beautiful hospice of St Cross in Winchester still gives the 'travellers' dole' of bread and ale – although with today's volume of tourism the total daily amount disbursed is limited to a gallon of ale. The old and sick were at first lodged in the monastery itself, but gradually a separate building evolved. The oldest surviving almshouse is that of St John's Hospital in Canterbury, founded by Lanfranc in 1084. Lazar houses, too, were established – but on the outskirts of towns, well away from the citizens, and it is for this reason that the surviving buildings are now found in suburbs, like the beautiful Lazar House in Norwich or St Nicholas' Hospital in Harbledown, on the main road about a mile from Canterbury.

After the suppression of the monasteries came a great wave of almshouse building, many of them founded by high-ranking prelates, like the splendid collegiate Whitgift's Almshouse in Croydon and Archbishop Abbot's Hospital in Guildford, built in 1619 and serving as Abbot's own home after his disgrace. The majority of these buildings were intended purely for local inhabitants, their founders' statutes making that very clear. 'It was the goode of Guildford – old Guildford as it was when I was borne, that I did seke,' Abbot emphasized, strictly limiting his hospitality to his fellow townsmen. But occasionally some benefactor would continue the tradition of hospitality to travellers. In Rochester Richard Watts established the Poor Travellers' Rest in 1579 'for six poor travellers who, not being rogues or proctors, may receive gratis for one night lodging, entertainment and four pence each'.

Charles Dickens visited the Travellers' Rest and left a scathing description of its finances:

I found that about a thirteenth part of the annual revenue was now expended on its (ostensible) purposes, the rest being handsomely laid out in Chancery, law expenses, collectors' tips, receivership, and other appendages of management, highly complimentary to the importance of the Six Poor Travellers.

Such common abuses in the administration of charities were first scrutinized, then checked by the various Charity Commissioners from the late nineteenth century onwards. Today there are some 23,000 almshouses, ancient and modern, run by a complex and very English system of co-operation between state and voluntary bodies. Each almshouse is run by its own board, under the eye of the Charity Commissioners and in accordance with the founders' intentions. Until the 1950s the inmates of most almshouses drew some kind of dole, whether in form of cash or kind, from the founder's endowments. Today, however, they will contribute anything up to £20 a week for their board and lodgings, which is treated as a contribution to maintenance, not rent, so meeting the legal definition of an almshouse as 'a corporate charity whose articles forbid it to charge rent'. The major qualification is still that of need, usually measured by the fact that the applicant is on Supplementary Benefit. The State is therefore contributing, via pensions and benefits, to their maintenance. But the upkeep of the almshouse itself – the roof over the residents' heads, the garden in which they walk, the common room where they maintain human contact – all these are paid for by the generosity of the long-dead founder. It would be an interesting actuarial exercise to calculate just how much the practical Christianity of the past is saving the government of the present.

6

Success to the Mayor

Edward, by the grace of God, king of England, lord of Ireland, and Acquitain, to his bishops, abbots, priors, earles, barons, justices, sheriffs, rulers, officers and all baylies and his faithful subjects. Know yee that we have for the furtherance of our towne of Guldeford and for the tranquility and quietness of the good men of the same towne, of our special grace granted, and by this our charter confirmed to the same men being tenants of the towne aforesaid, to sametowne with the appurtenances TO HAVE AND TO HOLD to them, their heirs, and successors, in feefarm of us and our heirs with all rents, yssues, profitts and emoluments which John Brocas, late keeper of the towne had . . . yielding therefore to us and our heirs at our exchequer every yeare tenn pounds . . .

So, in October 1366, the thousand or so citizens of Guildford in Surrey were informed, in a lengthy and curious admixture of noble sentiment and mercantile calculation, that their town had at last come of age after four centuries in which it had been considered a part of the Royal Manor of Guildford. King Edward III was, in fact, giving very little in hard cash to his faithful subjects in Guildford and he was giving it late. John Brocas, the last 'free farmer' of the town, had paid exactly double for the privilege of collecting the revenues of the manor and had complained that they were not worth the £20, even though his 'farm' or revenue area had included the royal castle and the royal park. These were specifically excluded from the charter: what the townsfolk were actually receiving were the taxes on brewers, tanners and butchers – a third of which went anyway to the Earl of Surrey – the profits of the local courts and the goods of criminals. But far more important than the actual cash value of the 'gift' was the theory of autonomy the town now possessed to collect its own revenues. By 'fee-farming' the town to its inhabitants the lord of the manor had commuted its total potential into a yearly cash rental – the gardens, the houses, the shops now belonged to the citizens. The lord of the manor here was also the all-powerful monarch and there was nothing in theory to prevent him bringing the town again under his direct power. Three hundred years later James II, in the last defence of absolute monarchy, did indeed withdraw the town's charters, together with all the others in the United Kingdom, and imposed his nominee to the town governance but his successor was in some haste to restore them. Charter rights might not possess the theological sanctions that the divine right was supposed to confer – but few kings were disposed to test their relative values by arbitrarily abrogating sworn promises and gifts.

The progress of the towns of England towards 'freedom' was the work of lawyers, not soldiers, accompanied by the clink of gold, not the rattle of steel. Money, or its equivalent in services and goods, underlies the relationship between all towns and their lord of the manor whether he was the local baron, or the distant king. That great survey of England called Domesday had one precise, pragmatic purpose: to establish who owned what and therefore how much he could afford to pay in cash, kind or services. Some of the towns combined payment in kind with that of cash: Thetford's fee farm included ten goat skins and four ox hides; Cirencester had to contribute 3000 loaves of bread; Norwich presented its monarch with a bear. Some of the seemlier or more adaptable payments of kind survived to become the 'quaint customs' beloved of antiquarians: Guildford still offers its visiting monarch a plum cake and a pair of gloves.

After the Norman Conquest the chief instrument of town government was the universally hated figure of the 'shire reeve' or sheriff. Matthew Paris describes one such with a pen dipped in venom: 'In this year [1268] died William Heron, sheriff of Northumberland, the hammer of the poor, passing – as we believe – from the thirst of avarice in the temporal world to the thirst of Tantalus in the nether region.' The sheriffs cheated and extorted as a matter of course: at Cambridge the sheriff taxed the citizens for the building of a stone bridge – and built a wooden bridge instead. He deliberately delayed the task of building in order to raise yet more money from the ferry he operated. It was the monarch himself who trimmed the sheriff down to size, keeping close watch upon his accounts and loading him with routine duties until it became an office unattractive to an ambitious man.

The king was prepared to sell anything to his loyal subjects except political power – nor were citizens particularly interested in acquiring it. The commune – that distinctive development on the Continent – never came into being: there is nothing here to compare with the quasi city-states of Bruges or Bordeaux. The charters were deliberately vague, leaving large areas undefined, frequently conferring blanket rights by simply referring to a similar charter granted to another town. But each charter marked, fractionally, the town's advance towards self-governance by the mayor.

The title 'mayor' for the first citizen of the town was borrowed from the French in the early thirteenth century, among the first recorded usages of the title being in Lincoln and Barnstaple in 1210. The mayor's status as first citizen was a by-product of his other, and far more important, role as head of the local guild of merchants. For, from the thirteenth century down to the nineteenth, the basis of the town's government was the guild, originally a religious organization but increasingly evolving into a craft body. It was the guild merchant, as the governing body was known, which ultimately inherited the town from the lord of the manor, running it as a closed society for the benefit of its members, presiding over its own court, governing the lives of the citizens down to the minutest detail. It discharged its functions efficiently enough until the inherent weakness of an inward-looking system produced that deterioration in control which led to the municipal reforms of 1835.

The concept of exclusion lay at the heart of the guild merchant. The smaller craft guilds of the town, whose masters formed the guild merchant, were exclusive enough but they could claim legitimately that they were concerned with upholding the standards of workmanship as well as reducing competition. The guild merchant existed only to trade, and the trading facilities of the town – the town itself – existed only for the benefit of guild members. 'No forayner of what craft soever shall use the mercate, unless by consent of the mayor and his brethren' was the point hammered home again and again, but exceptions had to be made. The immensely powerful international trading company known as the Hanseatic League is an obvious case in point. Their palatial quarters in King's Lynn rival the town's own guildhalls. But the League was in many ways unusual. Although it could put enormous pressure upon the towns with whom it designed to trade, its employees were virtually prisoners of commerce. In most towns they were sworn to celibacy, living a monastic life behind the high walls of their 'factory', forbidden to have any social contact with the natives. And by the early sixteenth century, the League was in decline, an English merchant gleefully recording 'most of their teeth have fallen out and the rest do sit but loosely in their heads'.

Strangers who were allowed to trade in the town bore the burden of almost crippling restrictions. They were obliged to bring their wares to a public place for inspection – a tactic the merchants of Wilton tried to use when seeking to divert traders from their rivals in Salisbury. They could not sell by retail: they were forced to yield first choice of any material in short supply to native guildsmen and were usually severely restricted to the amount of time they could stay in the town – rarely more than a month.

The guild merchant was, in theory, open to all members of the town but in practice it was run by a handful of rich men, frequently known as *probi homines*. The precise circumstances under which, legally, they were chosen are never very clear, but quite evidently they formed a self-perpetuating body with members moving up through various official roles to that of mayor.

The mayor enjoyed very considerable ceremonial honours, and a certain number of perquisites. But there was also provision for very substantial penalties should a man, on being elected, decline office as mayor or any other subsidiary office. The reluctance obviously stemmed from the heavy expenses connected with the honour of high office. The English institutionalized drunkenness. The mayor and other major officers were expected, as a matter of course, to feast their brethren on accepting office and on different occasions through the year. The custom, in various forms, proved remarkably tenacious. A late nineteenth-century mayor of Guildford recorded his disgust at the marathon banquet, followed by a prolonged drinking bout, which celebrated the mayor's inauguration. The custom perpetuated and exaggerated the tendency towards a small ruling class, for there was no point in electing a poor man who could neither pay for the feasting, nor afford the heavy fine in lieu.

The *probi homines* formed the corporation and it was they who elected, at an annual meeting of the guild merchant court, the officers of the guild. Parallel with this court in most towns was the Court Leet, the vernacular term for the *curia legalis* which had directly inherited the king's powers in the town. The business and powers of the two courts overlapped but, in general, the court of the guild merchant concerned itself with the financial and social business of the town appointing, among other officials, the bailiff and the hall warden – custodian of the guildhall and collector of guild fees – while the Court Leet appointed the various tasters – officials responsible for the control of food prices and qualities.

Certain areas fell outside the control of the mayor – monastic and royal establishments in particular. Winchester was particularly unfortunate for it had a monastery, a cathedral, the bishop's castle and palace, and the king's castle on the south side of the town: even in the northern section there was the Queen's house where she not only lived rent free, but also collected rent from a number of the stalls in the market. And to compound it all, the bishop held the right to all river tolls. Not surprisingly, Winchester faced severed financial problems. In 1450 the town claimed that 997 houses were empty and eleven streets were dilapidated and they pleaded for royal relief. They received scant comfort.

On their side, the townsfolk clung to the letter and spirit of their hard-gained liberties. In King's Lynn it was customary for the mayor to be preceded in procession by an official carrying a horn-tipped wand. When the Bishop of Norwich visited Lynn in 1377 he insisted that the wand be carried before him. The townsfolk responded violently, attacking the procession and breaking it up. Fifty years were to pass before the Bishop of Norwich again visited King's Lynn and it was then with a powerful bodyguard.

The picture presented by the town records is of a strongly coherent community with a corresponding lack of individual privacy, and of public control extending over a very wide field. Citizens were ordered to church as a matter of course both before and after the Reformation: in the Puritan era, in particular, innkeepers were fined for selling ale during divine service. The extent to which the local authority tried to control even minor matters is illustrated in *Bacon's Annals of Ipswich*, the sixteenth-century collection of town records: in one instance, for seventy years the corporation tussled with the problem of the pricing and ingredients of candles, edict following edict to close loopholes as fast as the butchers, who supplied the tallow, and the chandlers opened them.

The greater part of a town's trade was naturally concerned with supplying the everyday wants of citizens and travellers. An analysis of the town records of Norwich for the early part of the thirteenth century shows that there were 133 different trades in sixty-three guilds. Some have disappeared, their very names now mysterious – trades like ganyer, gelman, coner; others are highly specialized, like the pudding wife and the spoon-maker. But what is remarkable is that the vast majority of trades are flourishing in the twentieth century. They may have changed their form, or been absorbed into others, but the basic human needs as reflected in the thirteenth-century list of Norwich trades would be reflected in the stock-in-trade along any twentieth-century high street.

For centuries wool was the king of industries, creating with its ancillary trades vast wealth not only for individuals but for entire towns – and dragging down those towns when changes in marketing or fashion occurred. Out of the surplus wealth rose the splendid wool churches which now stand isolated in fields or towns that have dwindled beneath them. The prevalence of the symbol of the woolpack – as inn sign or as part of a town's arms – is an indication of the power of the fleece. England had been producing wool since the time of the Roman empire, but the great mediaeval wave began building up in the thirteenth century. It was wool which attracted the Hanseatic League to the country: wool which created the enormous wealth of many monasteries, so well were they geared to the rearing of sheep. At the time of the Conquest, Ely Abbey had 13,400 sheep; in 1259 the Bishop of Winchester farmed 29,000 head. Cirencester had ten immensely wealthy wool merchants in the early fourteenth century. The cloth merchants of Shrewsbury built their splendid half-timbered houses out of the profits of the monopoly they were able to establish for Welsh-made cloth.

The guilds tried to control the booming industry but with little success. The nature of the trade enabled both entrepreneurs and small independent artisans to by-pass the urban guilds. In particular the establishment of fulling mills in rural areas was a severe blow to many towns. In 1555 Bridgwater, Taunton and Chard in

Somerset combined to send a petition protesting against this dilution of labour. They complained to the Queen that hitherto these towns 'had been well and substantially inhabited maintained and upholden for the most part by the making of woolen clothes'. Now, however, 'certain persons dwelling in villages and hamlets, not being prentices, have of late days exercised, used and occupied the mysteries of cloth-making, weaving, fulling and shearing within their own house . . .' But the great industry made its own pace, formed its own pattern regardless of attempts to direct it into socially acceptable channels. In his mid-sixteenth century journey around England, John Leland noted that very many towns continued to owe their prosperity to wool – 'it standeth by clothing' is his frequent remark about a town – but they were by no means the same towns that had been waxing prosperous through wool a century or so earlier. He found Lincoln, which had once been famous for its cloths of scarlet and green, in a state of 'great and insuperable decay': twenty-four out of thirty-eight churches had been pulled down, so dilapidated had they become – a direct result of the local shift in the wool trade.

The guilds controlled the quality of their products but the two basic foods – bread and ale – were controlled by the town. The Assize of Bread was held weekly by the mayor, when the price would be fixed for the following seven days according to the prevailing price of wheat. The Assize of Ale similarly fixed the price of ale. Traditionally, quality of ale was judged by pouring a little on the seat of a chair on which the ale taster then sat: good quality ale should stick to his breeches, which were made of leather. Breaches of regulation were promptly punished by a fine, or by public exposure in stocks or pillory. Few pillories survive today, presumably because of the vulnerability of their long supporting pole, but the solid stocks are a feature of many towns: significantly, they are usually near the market cross, as at Oakham where an unusually tender corporation provided a shelter for the malefactor. Their use was declining by the nineteenth century. Cobbett in his 1820s tour was highly critical of those towns which allowed their stocks to be covered in weeds, evidence of a deplorably casual approach to the problem of law and order.

The right to try – and if necessary execute – its own malefactors varied from town to town. But even where that right was reserved to the king's justices, it was expected that execution should take place before the eyes of the townsfolk. Ludlow's street called Galdeford – Gallows Street – is a chilling reminder that the gallows was as much part of the town's furniture as the market cross. Defoe noted that the gallows at Guildford was placed on a hill 'so that the Towns People from the High Street may sit at their Shop Doors and see the Criminals Executed'. Worcester had five gallows, because five local lords held the 'gallows rights'. These could be a useful source of income: in 1285 the Abbot of Peterborough proved his right to retain £40 from the goods of felons in one year. In York, representatives of the king and the abbot took part in a macabre tussle over the body of a man the king's bailiff had hanged. The monks buried it in the monastery to establish gallows rights, the king's bailiff dug it up and rehanged it in chains.

If the town's progress towards legal – and what might be termed spiritual – independence is measured by the charters, its physical progress is measured by the increasing splendour of its 'town house'. 'Guildhall' and 'town hall' tend to be interchangeable terms, and in many towns the first did indeed evolve into the second, but, strictly speaking, they have separate functions. An excellent example of the guildhall proper is that of St George in King's Lynn. The guild was founded in 1376, received a royal charter in 1406 and erected the existing building probably between 1410 and 1420. The main hall is on the upper floor; below this hall, and at street level, is the vaulted undercroft for the storage of merchandise. After Edward VI dissolved the guilds in 1547 it ceased to function as such and, probably because King's Lynn possessed another guildhall – that of Holy Trinity – which in due course became the 'town' hall, that of St George continued to be used for non-municipal purposes.

Looking back down the long perspective of our urban history, it becomes evident that the 'town house' – the place where the town's identity is made manifest – developed in three or four main stages. The first stage is the archaic or *ad hoc* stage when the merchants made do with any building of adequate size, later adding perhaps a façade or other dignity to it. The guildhalls at Totnes and Guildford are good examples of this stage. Totnes's original guildhall – which survived until 1642 – was probably a single room with a bench round all four sides. In 1553, when the existing guildhall was built, the old one was described as 'so small that it is little suited and insufficient for the meeting of the aforesaid mayor and citizens'. Its successor occupied the site, probably adapted out of the refectory of the old priory – there is evidence that the sixteenth-century door pierces a wall of older date – and the granite pillars that give dignity to the little courtyard were later brought from the Church Walk. At Guildford, the main body of the guildhall resembles a large plain barn or market house given the dignity of stained glass and finally, in the 1680s, the splendid but rather deceptive Jacobean façade was added.

The second stage comes about during the seventeenth century when the citizens, aware of their identity, create a building which, while not so splendid as the continental *rathaus*, *hôtel de ville* or *palazzo municipale*, nevertheless reflects that civic pride: Abingdon's town hall belongs to this phase. This splendid building is quite unexpected in a town of this size – but wholly to be expected in a town possessing this degree of self-respect: students of urban history rapidly become aware how often Abingdon is cited to illustrate some point of urban development.

There were at least three 'market houses' in Abingdon before the foundation-stone of the existing building was laid in 1678. The builder is said to have been a Burford man, Christopher Kempster, but the design of the building has been, without documentary evidence, attributed to no less a hand than Christopher Wren's. Kempster carried out many commissions for Wren in London and Oxford and such a cachet would have stood him in good stead when the citizens were seeking a builder for their town hall. Not content with such a striking affirmation of civic dignity, in 1731 the corporation commissioned a splendid council chamber for the old municipal buildings that had been developed out of the old Hospital of St John. Altogether, Abingdon neatly illustrates the English ambivalence towards public functions, commissioning no less an architect than Wren for the town hall which was largely used for social occasions while being content to adapt – though adapting very handsomely – an existing building for its council debates.

Worcester's superb guildhall, whose present form is the product of the same period of civic pride as Abingdon's, is by contrast homogeneous both in history and function. It has always been, from the thirteenth to the twentieth century, the social heart of the town. The charter which Worcester received in 1227 gave it, among other privileges the right of establishing a guild merchant, and the first guildhall came into being as a result. It was a large, timber-framed building containing the courts of justice – with the notorious dungeon known as the Peephole, mentioned in Foxe's *Book of Martyrs*. It was replaced, in 1721, by the present building, the probable architect being Thomas White, a native of the city who had served his apprenticeship as a stone-cutter in London. He was made a Freeman of Worcester for carving the statue of Queen Anne which now occupies the niche over the main entrance of the guildhall. The statues of Charles I and Charles II, which complete the trio of monarchs on the front of this building, combining panache with dignity, are also probably White's work. There was a major extension of the building, under Gilbert Scott, during the 1870s and between them these two architects, separated by a century and a half, created a building that satisfies the bureaucratic demands of the twentieth century, while retaining the elegance of the eighteenth. And inside, the portraits reflect the continuity and homogeneity of the city's history with lots of loyal royal portraits – Charles I and II, Prince Rupert – but also the proud portrait of the first lady mayor.

On the other side of the country King's Lynn guildhall also continues as the heart of the town, mingling social, legal and civic roles. The present building, with its spectacular front of black and white chequered flints, was built in 1421: in 1980 it was proposed that the council remove its debates to the new, convenient and blandly meaningless 'council offices'. The proposal was emphatically rejected and King's Lynn governing body continues to meet in the good, solid oak council room where it always has met and where the portraits of the mayors brood over their deliberations. But it is below this chamber, in the massive vaulted undercroft, that King's Lynn, in a truly brilliant display of civic imagination, links past with present to emphasize continuance of identity in a shifting world. In January 1978 the Queen Mother opened what is now known as the Regalia Room, where the town's own crown jewels are on permanent and stunning display.

Every town has its regalia, that rather touching collection of chance-gathered treasures which are, in a very real sense, the family plate. Most regalia tend to have a rather tawdry, theatrical appearance but their significance transcends their appearance. Here is a wand given by Elizabeth I; flanking it might be two large, ugly rose bowls, or a basin and ewer given by some local Pomposo. The state sword is here and, of course, the maces which will be carried by tricorned officials on mayor-making day. And tucked into the various corners will be odds and ends of gifts made by citizens from time to time: the mayor's and mayoress's chains, a couple of salt cellars, a loving cup . . . Beauty they may not possess, but they have the powerful attraction of the family photograph album.

King's Lynn's permanent display, in crisp modern museum cases set against the ancient stonework, is civic pride at its best. But the treasures themselves are outstanding. Dominant is the great King John Cup of silver gilt and enamel, not quite as old perhaps as its name might indicate but almost certainly the oldest of its kind, made in the first half of the fourteenth century – an object that not only draws but holds the attention, for surely those exquisitely dressed men and women are fourteenth-century citizens of King's Lynn, immortalized in enamel and silver. The great Sword of State bears a tribute to Henry VIII on its cross-guard – but the scabbard has a portrait of Charles I, the town easily telescoping the centuries. Hanging on the walls is a rare, because totally unbroken, series of town charters from the very first granted by King John in 1204. And in a glass case is what must be Europe's – and hence, it is claimed, the world's – oldest paper book, the so-called Red Register dating from 1307 and recording the Assemblies of the Trinity Guild who once owned this guildhall.

The third stage of the development of the 'town's house' was the town hall proper, the extravaganza whose size was made necessary by the municipal reforms of the early nineteenth century, but whose ornaments are the product of the high noon of Victorian England. Chester's town hall, built almost on the site of the Roman *principia*, was opened in 1869 by Edward, Prince of Wales and Earl of Chester, a looming, gothic, grey sandstone building liberally supplied with allegorical and historic sculptures. Chester's elder sister, Colchester, received its town hall in 1902. The official guidebook says with truth, though with wryness: 'It has fewer friends than it deserves for its tower dominates the High Street and the skyline in a very happy manner.' It is perhaps fitting that England's oldest city should be one of the very few whose municipal palace, expression of the town's identity, beckons on the traveller when he is still far from the town, in the manner of its continental peers.

Norwich is another such. The City Hall of Norwich acts as a link between the last proud flowering of the urban impulse, and its transformation into the dull anonymity of the 'civic centre' or 'municipal offices' which characterize the seats of town government in the last quarter of the twentieth century. When, in the very depth of the Depression of the 1930s, Norwich courageously decided to replace its ancient, beautiful but now impracticable Guildhall with a twentieth-century equivalent, it turned to its Scandinavian origins for inspiration. The architects, James and Pierce, took Stockholm City Hall as model and created for Norwich a building that combines romanticism and functionalism: seen from afar at dusk, the great tower resembles a titanic cowled figure brooding over the city. But the interior is a disappointment. All majesty without, Norwich's city hall is all meanly bureaucratic within, a bewildering warren of anonymous rooms stacked together like egg-boxes, a fitting harbinger of the purely functional, cost-conscious, wholly anonymous municipal buildings that themselves reflect – in so far as purely negative forms can reflect – the current erosion of civic identity.

Stencilled in a great frieze along the front of Ripon's town hall is the proud legend 'Except Ye Lorde Keep Ye Cittie Ye Wakeman Waketh In Vain' – the Wakeman being the title for the town's chief citizen. But in the corridor of the same building, incised in imperishable stone, is one of the most grovelling acknowledgements of feudal dependence. The mayor and corporation acknowledge

the benefit conferred on the town by Mrs Elizabeth Allanson, late of Studley Royal who erected these buildings in 1799 and during her life permitted them to be used for the preservation of the muniments of the Corporation of Ripon and for holding the public meetings of the body . . .

They thanked the lady for a legacy of £300 which enabled them to light their streets and finished up by thanking yet another lady, Mrs Elizabeth Lawrence, for permitting them to put up this tablet thanking everybody in 1808. In other words, until the early nineteenth century Ripon was run by and through and largely for a number of wealthy local families, one of whom built the town house.

English town life was never disfigured by the ferocious battles between citizens and nobility which were a characteristic of so many continental towns, Italy in particular. Their interests were parallel, rather than conflicting for, in the main, the power-bases of the nobility lay deep in the country. James Rush, an ambassador of the infant United States of America in the eighteenth century, astutely put his finger on the matter. The aristocracy might have their houses in the large cities, London in particular, he said:

But their *homes* are in the country. Their turretted mansions are there with all that denotes perpetuity – heirlooms, family memorials, pictures, tombs. The permanent interests and affections of the most opulent classes centre almost universally in the country.

Many of the nobility were drawn to the towns for one reason or another, but carefully built just outside them. A writer in 1579 noted:

The manner of the most Gentlemen and Noble men also, is to house them selves (if possible they may) in the Subburbes of the Cittie, because moste commonly, the ayre there being somewhat at large, the place is healthy and through the distance from the bodye of the Towne, the noyse is not so much.

And, of course, they avoided any embarrassing discussions regarding jurisdiction and the payment of taxes. The Duke of Somerset, when he built his halfway house between London and Petworth, placed it quite literally within inches of Guildford's town boundary.

The great mansion of Petworth is one of the few to be built

physically as part of a town. Cobbett's description of it in 1823
held true until the suburban explosion of the 1920s: 'Lord Egre-
mont's house is close to the town, and with its outbuildings garden
walls and other erections is, perhaps, nearly as big as the town:
though the town is not a very small one.' Despite his radical
leanings, Cobbett nevertheless quite approved, for the town could
not but benefit from the proximity of a good landowner. The
citizens of Stamford, on the other hand, seemed to have gained
little from being neighbours of the mighty Lord Burghley, whose
house Burghley House on the edge of the town left Defoe agog: 'It
looks more like a town than a house: the towers and the pinnacles
so high, and placed at such a distance from one another, look like
so many distant parish churches in a great town.' Stamford was
going through a pretty bad time when William Cecil, Lord Burghley, began building his vast house. The fashion in wool clothing
had changed, the Welland was silting up and Stamford appeared
to be a dying city. Apart from the employment provided for masons
and, later, domestic servants and provisioners, the existence of
Burghley Park had no particular effect on the life of the town
despite the fact that it was, in Defoe's words, 'the Property, as it
may be called, of the Earles of Exeter'.

Relationships between towns and their neighbouring nobility
and gentry were, however, in the main mutually beneficial and
amiable. Ripon was by no means the only town to owe its principal
public building to a rich philanthropist. Amersham's Market House
was given to the town by the Drake family in 1682 and the Earl of
Onslow contributed to the building of Guildford's guildhall. The
upward movement which marked English society from the Tudor
period onward further blurred the distinction between 'citizen' and
'nobleman' and the man who had arrived still felt the strong pull of
urban patriotism. The rich Hugh Clopton of Stratford, in Leland's
description 'having never wife nor children converted a great part
of his substancy in good works in Stratford, first making a
sumptuous new bridge and arch of stone'. Peter Blundell of
Tiverton left a large part of his estate of £40,000 to founding the
famous grammar school in the town.

Nobility and townsfolk had particular reason to court each other
in the matter of representation to the seat of government. After

their emancipation, those towns which had been governed directly on behalf of the king by the official called the Seneschal lost their friend at court in exchange for gaining their own mayor. Later, the creation of the office of High Steward or Lord Lieutenant for the County established a link. And as the importance and influence of parliament grew, so citizens and gentry sought to make use of each other. Some towns objected strongly to the virtual usurpation of urban representation at parliament by the nobility: others – probably most – were either resigned to it as a fact of life, or actually preferred that a nobleman should shoulder the onerous financial burden of parliamentary representation. Charles Dickens portrayed, in the liveliest possible fashion, what was the view of probably the majority of ordinary 'voters' when he described the 'election' at Eatanswill in *The Pickwick Papers*. The town was probably Bury St Edmunds – 'In Mr Pickwick's notebook we can just trace an entry of the fact that the places of himself and followers were booked by the Norwich Coach'. The candidates were the Honourable Samuel Slumkey of Slumkey Hall and Horatio Fizkin Esq of Fizkin Lodge, and the 'electorate' had no other interest in the contest except what could be squeezed out of the candidates in the shape of eatables, drinkables and hard cash.

A last faint echo of the thousand-year-old story occurs occasionally with the sale at auction of manorial rights. These are the deeds which give legal right to certain archaisms such as the right to appoint a pinder, or collector of stray cattle, the right to hold a Court Leet or appoint a town crier. An Essex solicitor, John Beaumont, collected more than eighty of these and after his death his widow raised more than £50,000 by selling them. Most buyers are activated by historic curiosity – or perhaps even vanity, for possession of the deed allows the buyer to refer to himself as lord of the manor of X and sign Esq after his name. But occasionally the antique rights have lively modern value, particularly when they refer to market rights. Markets are almost invariably run today by the local authorities who are sometimes obliged to defend their 'usurpation' against a lord of the manor appearing out of the mists of history, armed with a parchment document. And with growing interest in the past, the deeds achieve antiquarian value. In 1977 Lord Kinnoull tried to promote a parliamentary bill to forbid the sales of lordships to foreigners. A Chicago trading stamp company had offered the lordship of the manor of Felsham and Drinkstone for the equivalent of £800 worth of trading stamps. Lord Kinnoull's peers, less moved than himself by this *lèse-majesté*, declined to turn his bill into law. A meat-packer in the New World may well therefore be lord of the manor in whose demesne lies one or other of our ancient towns.

7
The Citizen at Play

At about 8.45 on any fine evening in Ripon a small crowd begins to gather around the base of the elegant eighteenth-century obelisk in the market square. A little before 9 P.M. a figure, wearing a tricorn hat and carrying a great curved horn slung from a baldrick, materializes from among the cars parked in the square and walks towards the obelisk. He takes up his stance facing the town hall that is emblazoned with that proud motto and, as the minute hand of the town hall clock moves up to the hour, he puts the mouthpiece of the great horn to his mouth and begins to pump air into the instrument, much as a bagpiper fills the instrument's bladder. Precisely as the clock touches the hour, the Wakeman sounds his horn.

The sound of the horn is, in fact, rather unimpressive – barely audible above the traffic. What is impressive – indeed, well-nigh incredible but attested from every source – is that every night for over a thousand years the Wakeman of Ripon has set the watch in this manner and at this place nightly without a break. The time occasionally changes – during World War II it took place at 6 P.M. – but never the event. Currently the Wakeman receives £1 a night and 50p petrol allowance – part of his duty is to sound the watch outside the Mayor's house, which could be anywhere within miles of the market place. There is a Deputy Wakeman to help maintain that ceremony on 365 days a year, and by a quirk of history the current deputy is a young American computer expert working with NATO and living in Ripon. 'It causes some arguments with my wife when I have to dash out when we're entertaining, perhaps, but what an experience!'

The ceremony of the Ripon Wakeman is the most famous, because the oldest, of England's urban ceremonies. But behind the bland, anonymous face of many a 'developed' town, near the multi-storey car park or in front of the supermarket or down by the bus station, ceremonies centuries old take place unselfconsciously. In a remarkable book of photographs entitled *Once a Year* the photographer Homer Sykes caught many of these customs; and what is plainly evident from them is how involved and unselfconscious are the participants. Sometimes the elders, dressed up in ceremonial costume, look as though they might be aware of their significance but, curiously and encouragingly, it is the young – casually dressed in the classless, dateless clothes of current fashion, enthusiastically clutching the alcohol that figures in so many of the customs – who provide the dynamic as though it were a purely commonplace affair. And what is also evident is the renaissance of many a custom that was defunct in the early years of this century but which, in conscious reaction against the anonymizing process of modern urban life, has been reactivated.

The customs which survive today appear as colourful playlets, or pageants, which have no apparent relevance to anything outside themselves. Each, however, is the physical survival of a once vitally important corporate activity that either expressed the town's sense of identity, or helped it to govern itself. Beating the bounds, for example – today a light-hearted means of passing an hour or so – was once the means of establishing in the minds of an illiterate citizenry the extent of the town's jurisdiction. The Wareham Court Leet is an excellent example of an entire procedural system which has somehow survived, though all its externals are now directed towards entertainment. Court leets were those means whereby the lord of the manor regulated certain vital aspects of the town's life, in particular relating to tithes and quality of food-stuffs. Every November the Court Leet continues to meet in the town of Wareham in Dorset. Its only real function is the letting of grazing rights on Wareham Common but thereafter the constable, bailiff, ale-taster and the rest of the Court sit in solemn judgment on the quality of the town's ale and bread, and the cleanliness of its chimneys, invariably finding all wanting.

The symbolism that pervades the customs formed a vital role in a largely illiterate society. Superficially, the tussle between the Bishop of Norwich and the citizens of King's Lynn as to whether or not he should be preceded by a horn wand seems puerile – until it is realized that it was a symbol of authority, as potent in itself as the wearing of a crown. The significance of much of the symbolism has today been lost, but the original impetus remains. At High Wycombe, almost entirely swamped in modern development, the incoming and outgoing mayors (and their wives if willing) are solemnly weighed by the Chief Inspector of Weights and Measures. The Beadle then announces the weights, comparing them with the weights registered the previous year. Why? As with all such customs origins are uncertain or distorted. The popular assumption in High Wycombe is that an outgoing mayor who has increased in weight is assumed to have grown fat through sloth. At Ripon, the new mayor has to be 'hunted in' to office – much as the Speaker of the House of Commons is expected to show reluctance to take up his onerous task: the Ripon ceremony is doubtless a survival of the custom of penalizing any alderman who declined to accept office. At Abingdon, the inhabitants of one particular locality, Ock Street, have their own private mayor-making ceremony in June. The Mayor of Ock Street is elected by ballot and invested with his own regalia, including the 'Ock Street horns'. The custom supposedly began in the eighteenth century when, after an ox-roasting in the street, two groups of young men fought for the horns – but the custom bears so close a relationship to the Abbots Bromley Horn Dance that its origins must go back centuries earlier.

The Hungerford Hocktide is an elaborate variant of the Wareham Court Leet. The Berkshire town possesses some 200 acres of common land, to which certain citizens have the rights of grazing and fishing. A version of 'Hocktide', 'Tutti-day', gives a clue to the significance of the day-long custom that has developed, for 'tutti' derives from 'tithe', the Hocktide ceremony evidently being related to the distribution of valuable rights of tenure. At 8 A.M. on the second Monday after Easter the town crier summons all Commoners to the Hocktide Court. Here are elected the two officials who particularly take the public fancy, the Tithing Men or Tutti Men. Carrying flower-bedecked staves, theirs is the enjoyable task of making the round of all 'common right houses', collecting a kiss from the lady of the household and giving an orange in exchange. The day proceeds with a variety of other customs which have evidently been grafted on to the central ritual, and include the election of traditional officers – ale-tasters, hay-wardens and the like, as well as the Keeper of the Keys of the Common Coffer.

This contains a hunting horn, reputed to have belonged to John of Gaunt who is associated with the Commoners' rights.

Other rites derived from the Church's calendar, many of them taking place at or around Easter. The Pancake Bell is rung on Shrove Tuesday at midday in Scarborough to usher in a half-day's strenuous activity, in which skipping predominates. At Ashbourne in Derbyshire and St Colomb in Cornwall on the same day, violence has been canalized in a free-for-all ball game. In Ashbourne the Up'ards (those living north of the Henmore Stream) contend with the Down'ards (those living south) in an attempt to place a leather ball in the goal in each other's territory. At St Columb, the contenders are Town and Country, struggling for possession of the Silver Ball.

The Byzant ceremony in Shaftesbury relates to that ancient problem of the town's water-supply. The Byzant itself is an extraordinary object, now housed in the little private museum of Shaftesbury, and somewhat resembling a large vase or candlestick decked all over with feathers, ribbons and jewels – the whole currently being valued around £2000. 'On the first Sunday after Holy Cross Day' the mayor and townspeople descend the steep hill to Ensmore Green, carrying the Byzant as earnest of their right to use the springs of Ensmore Green. The lord of the manor welcomes the procession at 1 P.M., dancing follows and then the mayor's presentation of 'a pair of gloves, a calfs head and a gallon of ale'. In 1830 the then lord of the manor allowed the ceremony to be discontinued as the town felt that the expense of £30 was too great. But what in the nineteenth century was regarded as burden, in the twentieth is valued as a tradition, and in recent years the Byzant ceremony has been restored as a local fête.

The now retired Norwich Snap and the still vigorously flourishing Padstow Hobby Horse, or 'Oss, belong to an older and more mysterious past. Snap, a splendid dragon in green and gold, used to take part in the Lord Mayor's procession, designed so that one man could carry him. The procession was discontinued in the early part of this century and Snap retired to the museum; although the procession has been reinstated in recent years, there has been no move to bring Snap back. The 'Oss is a May-day character. Stabled at Padstow's Golden Lion inn, he is brought out during the morning and dances to energetic drum and accordion music. Like Snap, part of his duty is to harry young girls – and there is something about the extraordinary creature that sets up tension among most onlookers.

A major problem which faces towns that possess picturesque customs is that they run the risk of becoming tourist fodder. Padstow, in particular, is paying the price of simultaneously possessing such a custom, and being in a holiday area. In a letter to the present writer, an indignant resident described the result:

One event in particular is perhaps significant in illustrating the resentment felt by locals of tourists vulgarising the community's way of life. Padstow celebrates a very ancient Celtic Spring fertility rite each year on 1 May. This most moving occasion is not one at which Padstovians particularly welcome the vast crowds which now appear to be inevitable. Last year 1 May fell on a Bank Holiday. The crowds poured in, jamming the town solid and blocking every approach road for several miles. The traditional dancing by the Horse and participation by the locals was made virtually impossible by the sheer mass of humanity. Padstow was extremely angry, and many voiced their opinion that the ceremony should be discontinued for a year or so to allow the public to forget about it and then restarted without publicity. A sad fate for a domestic rite that has been observed without break for several hundred years.

The writer's hope that the 'Oss might dance again without publicity is almost certainly doomed to disappointment. The very factors that lead to the revival of town customs – that persuade the hard-headed Leicester Borough Council actually to create the office of town crier – will ensure that all picturesque customs will more and more be swamped in the tide of tourism.

Customs as enacted today are performed purely for entertainment. In tracking them back to their origins, it is virtually impossible to say where entertainment starts, and the deeper significance of the custom stops, the very large part played by drinking further helping to blur the distinction. The Mystery Plays of Chester undoubtedly had their roots in religion – in effect, transferring the drama of the high altar to the street – but the social spin-off must have been as important. The cycle took place at the feast of Corpus Christi (still a major social-cum-religious event in Catholic countries) and was later shifted to Whitsun. They were peripatetic by nature, the plays being performed on splendid carts, each of the craft guilds who performed striving to outdo the rest in the magnificence of their production and staging.

The Norwich Pageants lacked the literary polish of the Chester plays and so the dialogue has not survived, but the records show that, as in Chester, the entire town in the form of the guilds took part, each being allocated a particular role, thus: Mercers, Haberdashers: *Creation of the world*; Grocers, Raffemen: *Paradys*; *Hell carte* was the responsibility of no less than nine guilds – a decidedly mixed lot, including Glaziers and Wheelwrights; Dyers, Calenderers and Goldsmiths were responsible for *The birth of Christ with shepherdes and iiij Kynges off Colen* (presumably kings of Cologne); the Bakers, Brewers and Innkeepers sailed *Noyse Shipp* and so on, with the important guild of Worsted Weavers having the solitary honour of representing *The Holy Gost*. In Norwich, the religious impulse was in due course easily canalized into the civic with the development of the splendid Lord Mayor's procession or pageant. A handsome folio volume, published in 1855 shortly after the processions had ended, gives some idea of the sheer colour of the official party. The mayor, sheriff, town clerk, speaker, sword-bearer and mace-bearers are all well costumed. But it is the two standard bearers who attracted the attention, one in rose-pink and one in blue with matching standards. The procession was led by the delightfully named whiffler, dancing ahead with his inflated pig's bladder, clearing a path for the mayor. Shakespeare knew of him, referring to a character of *Henry V* 'Like a mighty whiffler before the king, seeming to prepare the way'. When Will Kemp danced from London to Norwich in 1599 the Corporation, as a signal mark of honour, sent whifflers to meet him, and the name at least survives still as a byline for a columnist in the local newspaper. As in other cities, whifflers, Snap, standard-bearers and all were swept away after the Municipal Reform Act of 1835. The Lord Mayor's procession was restored by the Chamber of Commerce in 1976 and proved immensely popular. But none of the old figures have as yet been revived, the procession more resembling the mechanized carnival which has become widespread, with floats contributed by, and illustrating activities of, local groups. Yet oddly enough, though the floats are mechanized and their subjects secular, they go back unconsciously to the pageant with its *Hell carte* manned by Glaziers and the rest.

It is now a commonplace that the early mystery plays and pageants gave birth to the Elizabethan theatre and all that followed. And the midwife was the inn. It would have been a natural progression for the actors to seek shelter from England's uncertain climate, and the inn-yard with its ready-made arena was an obvious place – a move which the landlord would have heartily encouraged. The great George in Southwark is the last of our galleried inns. Tucked behind a nondescript gate, side by side with a railway siding, the inn brings a breath of the country town into the roaring heart of London and in summertime the plays put on in the yard establish an unselfconscious link with the formative years of one of the world's greatest dramatic forms.

Physically, the English inn is having a very bad time. In the last third of the twentieth century, the hand of the brewer is lying as heavy upon it as the hand of the restorer lay upon the church in the corresponding period of the nineteenth century. It is perhaps invidious to pick one emasculated pub out of thousands but the Black Bull in Haworth, where Branwell Brontë drank his life away, can stand as representative for the rest. 'It used to be a real Yorkshire pub,' a local mourned. 'Stone floors, little wooden rooms. Now it could be somebody's bedroom: all pink velvet and shaded lights.' Even the Civic Trust uttered the discreet hope that some day it could be returned to its former condition.

Yet it must be recorded, too, that for the first time since the creation of our weird licensing system (which, in the words of the Chairman of the English Tourist Board 'treats adults like children and children like dogs') the pubs of England are again playing a full social role. The reaction against the excesses of the nineteenth century, taking advantage of war-time regulations in World War I, succeeded only in turning the inns into places where people went to get drunk for there was nothing else to do in them. Now, with the provision of meals and hot drinks, the admission of children (though under conditions which make them appear like animals with contagious diseases) and even the provision of live entertainment, the inn is coming back into its own.

The inn and the church are the twin poles around which the life of the town has revolved for centuries. But where the history of the individual church will have been recorded again and again in pedantic detail, the story of its ancient neighbour will be garbled, fragmented. Even our ambivalent names for the organization – inn, tavern, pub, hotel – are indicative of the complex role it plays in social life and the ambivalence with which it is regarded.

What is our oldest town inn? Any number claim the honour. The Angel in Grantham, on the Great North Road, can point to a strong tradition that King John used it as his court while in the town in 1213 – but the Fountain at Canterbury has traditions going back to 1029. The Old Fighting Cocks at St Albans has always had the strongest claim with a date of A.D.795 – but the Talbot at Oundle has recently entered the lists with a claim that 'it originates from A.D.638 when a group of monks founded it as a hostel'. Depending on what evidence is used – first recorded appearance, oldest part of the building, tradition – among the 'oldest' are the George at Salisbury (1320); the Maid's Head at Norwich (1287); the Salutation Inn, Nottingham (1240); the Bell at Finedon (1042).

The Talbot's claim, while strong, could be applied to any number of inns for there is little doubt that the English inn is yet another off-shoot of monasticism. The guest house of a monastery is usually a building separate from the monastery itself and the natural place to erect it would be on the town side of the monastery. The expertise to run such a place would develop, equally naturally, into the expertise required to run an inn. The beautiful George and Pilgrims in Glastonbury, rebuilt in 1455, gives evidence of its function in its name, but others are hidden. The first reference to the King's Head in Aylesbury in 1455, describes it as being 'three messuages called the Kyngeshede' when it apparently consisted of a shop, a cellar and a cottage. But it was undoubtedly built nearly a century before when the Greyfriars monastery was founded in Aylesbury in 1386. The shape of the refectory is still evident in the modern lounge, with its superb fifteenth-century window.

The King's Head is tucked away in a courtyard whereas the splendid George at Stamford, like the Angel at Grantham, is an excellent example of the wayside inn that has made a living by netting travellers as they passed along the road. The road is the

Great North Road, and the George would have been an early example of 'ribbon development': certainly its venerable 'gallows' sign, arrogantly stretched across the road, would not today be accepted by any conscientious town planner. The inn at the town gate, ready to offer hospitality to the tardy traveller who has found himself locked out, is a similar development: the Wheatsheaf at Ludlow, tucked up against Broad Gate, is one of these.

The inn, as much as the church, is the product of slow centuries of change, but where devoted students of ecclesiastical architecture seek to identify every point of change, the inn tends to be dismissed as Tudor or Victorian or vaguely 'mediaeval', though its cellars might be tenth-century and its rafters seventeeth-century while the rooms and furnishings cover all the intermediate and succeeding centuries. Much of the panelling of the residents' lounge at the Talbot in Oundle came from nearby Fotheringhay Castle. In filial rage, James I demolished the castle which had witnessed the execution of his mother, Mary, Queen of Scots, and the canny neighbours hastened to acquire the valuable fittings. The staircase at the Talbot is almost certainly that which Mary descended on the day of her execution. The present Angel at Bury St Edmunds, which occupies one side of the market square which Abbot Baldwin laid out is, in fact, composed of three separate inns, the first of which dates from 1452. Charles Dickens stayed here when he gave one of his exhausting readings at the Athenaeum next door. His rather dark little room with its four-poster is still kept in memory of him, but not as a shrine: any traveller may use it. The Crown at Bawtry has what is quite clearly an external eighteenth- or early nineteenth-century bow window *inside* the eighteenth-century front; nobody knows why – though they will tell you that Dick Turpin rode up the steps.

The town inns received a tremendous boost in the eighteenth century, first with the establishment of the mail-coach services and then, from the 1820s onwards, with the fast, efficient stage-coach. This is the transport that figures in endless Christmas cards but it is doubtful if those who used it were particularly aware of its romantic possibilities. A writer in the *Illustrated London News* in 1844 praised the wonderful new rail transport: 'We are not of those who regret the "good old coaching days" and "the roadside inn" ... Who for one instant would compare the trouble and extortions of the old coachyard to the comfort of the station.' But they brought trade to the town and guests, no matter how unwilling, to the inn. The coachmaster was an entrepreneur, controlling several hundred employees and several coaches. His first necessity in the towns on his route was a yard: he simply obtained one of the larger inns and adapted it to his purpose. It had to be large, for he could be working anything up to fifty coaches. Only a few would be in the home-yard at any one time, but they needed spare parts, maintenance, stabling and fodder. And the passengers, with only a short time to snatch a hasty meal, were at the landlord's mercy as the invective of many a traveller makes clear. It is from this period that the post houses and stage-coach inns acquire their characteristic high archway and yard surrounded by small rooms, where the travellers were relieved of cash in exchange for negus or a hasty chop.

But what the road bestowed, the railway took away. The new transport system swept the traveller – and the potential client of the inn – through the land at high speed. No longer was there need for coaching inns every few miles. The inns decayed, morally and physically, becoming mere drinking shops. It was at this stage that Earl Grey came to the paradoxical conclusion that a campaign to restore the inn to its old role would be a valuable contribution to the temperance movement. He proposed to the Lord-Lieutenants of the counties that each county should found its own Public House Trust which would restore those inns that had architectural value, while superintending their running. Out of this was born, in 1904, the Trust House movement which over the next thirty years acquired dozens of England's oldest inns. The Trust was fortunate in attracting not only competent managers for the individual houses, but enthusiastic and imaginative architects to restore years of neglect. When the ancient Red Lion at Colchester was stripped of its squalid plaster front it was found to be a jewel of fifteenth-century carved woodwork. At Shrewsbury, a large room at the Lion which had been used as a commercial stockroom, proved to be a ballroom designed by the Adam brothers; panelling stripped from the White Swan at Stratford displayed a series of murals of 1560. The Trust House movement, inspired by a temperance campaigner, undoubtedly saved some of England's most beautiful and historic inns.

In 1931 the journalist Thomas Burke, in a sprightly book on the inn, prophesied its almost immediate demise.

The pub is already doomed and will be replaced by the social club or Continental café and the inn will quickly follow, speed will kill it. Those old inn-yards that were built for mail and stage-coaches, though they have been cleverly transformed into garages, have never been really suitable to that business and they will, of course, be utterly useless when the plane takes over from the car.

Time has a habit of creating ironies: the railway has succumbed to its ancient predecessor, the road, the plane has not taken over and the inns have benefited – if at the price of islanding themselves in asphalt car parks.

On 25 April 1942 German bombers appeared over Bath on their Baedeker tour of England. Among the architectural victims of the visitation were the Assembly Rooms built by John Wood in 1770 at a cost of £14,000. The building was reduced to a shell and the National Trust – who had owned it since 1931 – was faced with the problem that faced so many owners of bombed historic buildings: rebuild and restore, or demolish and build for twentieth-century needs. The War Damage Commission resolved the argument by offering compensation based on restoration. In 1946 the architect Sir Albert Richardson accepted the commission and, basing his work on photographs, drawings and documentary evidence, he recreated the Assembly Rooms as they had been in their heyday. And, despite the opinion of sceptics who felt that such a building had no role to play in the twentieth century, it proved remarkably successful.

The Assembly Rooms were the middle- and upper-class equivalent of the tavern. When Cyrus Bantam, Master of Ceremonies at Bath, welcomed Mr Pickwick to the Assembly Rooms he very properly emphasized their class distinction:

This is a ball night. The ball nights in Ba-ath are monuments snatched from Paradise; rendered bewitching by music, beauty, elegance, etiquette and – and – and above all by the absence of trades people, who are quite inconsistent with Paradise; and who have an amalgamation of themselves at the Guildhall which is, to say the least, remarkable.

The Bath Assembly Rooms were financed by private subscribers who appointed a committee. In addition to the building costs, each subscriber was called upon to pay £60 for the furnishing of the Rooms. The only items of the original furnishings which survive today are the nine great chandeliers, purchased for the then very considerable sum of £999. The standard of furnishing can perhaps be assessed by the apportioning of the War Damage Commission's compensation, of which £60,000 was used for the constructional work – but £300,000 for the interior. Many of the details of the present building can be identified from the description in the 1772 *Bath Guide*:

The entrance into these rooms for [sedan]-chairs is on the west side under a portico of the Doric order, from whence three doors open into a hall, in the centre of which hangs a chandelier ... From the hall through an octagon ante-chamber, which has four marble chimney pieces and a cupola richly ornamented, the company are led into the grand ballroom by an avenue to the left, to the concert or card-room on the left and to the tea-room on the right.

The first Master of Ceremonies (forerunner of the egregious Cyrus Bantam) was a Captain William Wade who laid down stringent rules as to dress, decorum and class of visitor of which Cyrus Bantam himself would have approved.

The Rooms lost their popularity in the late nineteenth century, reflecting Bath's own decline as the sea-side resorts began to rival the spas. In 1903 the Committee staved off financial disaster by selling Gainsborough's portrait of Captain Wade but later the ubiquitous cinema took over the ballroom which Rowlandson had made famous, and most of the furniture was sold in 1920. Conservation in the 1920s being decidedly a minority interest, the future of the Rooms would have been problematical, to say the least, had they not been bought by the Society for the Protection of Ancient Buildings. They were given to the National Trust who, in turn, let them to Bath City Council at a nominal rent, on condition of their being restored. This was done, at a cost of £30,000, and the Rooms were reopened in October 1938: less than four years later they were destroyed in the air raid.

The story of the Assembly Rooms at Bath is fairly representative of similar organizations throughout the country: the establishment by an exclusive group in the eighteenth century, early success followed by long decline, restoration by civic philanthropists – and the discovery, to the surprise of most, that such 'citizens' drawing rooms' play a valuable and active role in the twentieth century. Thomas Ivory's beautiful Assembly Rooms in Norwich followed a similar pattern. In 1754 a group of prominent citizens of Norwich signed a covenant 'to form an entertainment centre for assemblies, cards, plays and bowls' by converting a historic town house, Chapply Field House, into the fashionable Assembly Rooms. They were opened in 1775 and functioned – including among their 'brilliant occasions' the Trafalgar Ball on the occasion of Nelson's victory – until 1856 when they were sold off. The Rooms subsequently became a masonic hall, a girls' school – and, during World War II, a camouflage school under the direction of Oliver Messel. After the war it was acquired by a local businessman and, under the direction of one of the architects of the City Hall, it was restored and again functions as its creators intended.

In Bury St Edmunds the New Assembly Rooms were developed out of a seventeenth-century house an Angel Square and survived in that form until the early nineteenth century. In 1854, the splendidly named Athenaeum Literary Institute took the building over, changed its frivolous name to The Athenaeum, invited Charles Dickens to lecture there (when he stayed at the Angel on the other side of the square) and in general gave a more portentous tone to eighteenth-century frivolity. Like its companions in Bath and Norwich, the Athenaeum, too, discharges a unique role in its parent town – a small but beautiful building acting as a social catalyst, for meetings and functions of every kind are still held there.

The mid-century transformation of the Bury Assembly Rooms into the Bury Athenaeum was very much a thing of its day, symptomatic of the change to earnestness, self-help and moral goals that characterized so much of Victorian England. It took form particularly in the tide of self-education that was sweeping the country and would, in due course, produce those education, museum and public library Acts which would have such enormous consequences. One far-reaching aspect of this movement was that of the Mechanics' Institutes which, born in Glasgow in 1823, rapidly established themselves in almost every English town. By 1850, there were at least 700 Institutes: today there are about twenty, the activities of the majority having been absorbed by the state-organized cultural bodies. The buildings they put up so proudly for themselves have either been taken over by the state – such as the Wakefield Mechanics' Institute, which is now the Museum, or Skipton's, now the public library – or they have been demolished, not possessing those favoured signs of 'antiquity' which a local authority will recognize as earning stay of execution. In a letter to the present writer the Secretary of the Berkhamsted Institute remarked with some bitterness: 'The Institute continued to occupy rooms in the Town Hall building until 1972, when the Council intended to modernize the building but subsequently left the property to rot.' As the Institute was itself largely responsible for the erection of the town hall in 1860, the bitterness is understandable.

The course of events at Berkhamsted is typical of most. The town had a population of 3000 when, in September 1845, eleven townsmen met and decided to form a local Institute. In their recruiting drive, George Cruikshank was characteristically generous, travelling to the town to address meetings. As one of the founding members recorded:

The result was a large accession of members. Berkhamsted was highly favoured by the residence of a number of gentlemen of wealth and influence, some of them possessing considerable literary and scientific ability who, almost without exception, placed their services at the disposal of the Society.

A reading room was established, classes and lectures in astronomy, literature, mesmerism and political economy launched: there was even an ambitious plan to establish a museum, stocked for the most part, it would seem, with stuffed kangaroos, flying squirrels and flying mice supplied by a townsman who had made good in Australia. In 1945, the Institute's centenary year, it had every hope of survival but by the late 1970s it was, for all practical purposes, dead.

Initially the purpose of the Institutes was 'the instruction of mechanics in the principles of the art they practise as well as in other branches of useful knowledge', but by the end of the century they had largely been taken over by and for the middle classes. The Wakefield Institute (whose Honorary Librarian had been George Gissing's father) had 244 'working class' members out of a total membership of 775 in 1883, according to an analysis made by its historian, Clifford Brooke. At the turn of the century the Guildford Institute counted among its presidents the Earl of Onslow, the Duke of Northumberland and a Lord Chief Justice. This institute was one of the very few to survive, in the building it had erected for itself, into the twentieth century. In 1981 it became part of the University of Surrey, though still maintaining its identity, an unusual example of urban symbiosis.

In 1830 William Cobbett noted:

One of the great signs of the poverty of people in the middle rank of life is the falling off of the audiences at the playhouse. There is a playhouse in almost every country town where the players used to act occasionally, and in large towns almost always. In some places, they have of late abandoned acting altogether. In others, they have acted, very frequently, to no more than ten or twelve persons. I have heard of one manager who has become a porter to a warehouse.

Over the next century, the fortunes of the country theatre rose and fell. Most were dependent upon travelling companies like that controlled by the actor-manager Henry Thornton, who had a circuit in the south-east based on small profits, quick returns and the very minimum of expenditure. The managements of these small but vigorous entrepreneurs are irresistibly reminiscent of that of Vincent Crummles, complete with endless 'final benefits', child prodigies and advertisements for low comedians.

The very similar chronology of three separate theatres at Stamford, Richmond in Yorkshire, and Bury St Edmunds show the influences that were at work. The beautiful Georgian theatre in Richmond was opened in 1788, closed during the 1840s – about the time that Cobbett noted the effect of middle-class penury –

and for the next century was used as a wine cellar. In 1963 it was restored and re-opened and is, in the opinion of Alec Clifton-Taylor, 'the best preserved and without question the most authentic Georgian theatre in the country'. Stamford's theatre was built in 1768 – by a combination of a master builder and a comedian – was closed, restored and re-opened in 1849; closed again at the end of the century and for the next seventy years or so survived as a club and public hall. In 1976 a major restoration brought the theatre back to life as part of the Stamford Arts Centre.

Bury's theatre began life in the Market Cross. Its lessee, William Wilkins (later the architect of the National Gallery) had an interest in the Norwich circuit of players who included Bury on their round through Cambridge, Ipswich, Colchester and Yarmouth. The little theatre was very successful and Wilkins, raising a capital of £5000, founded the New Theatre which was opened in 1819. Like those at Stamford and Richmond, it ran into difficulties in the 1840s, closed, re-opened in 1845 and somehow staggered on until 1925. For forty years thereafter it was used as a barrel store by the local brewery. In 1959 a local campaign to restore it raised £37,000, the brewers agreed to lease the building to the National Trust for 999 years, and in 1965 the Theatre Royal, Bury St Edmunds, again opened its doors to the public.

In 1943, as the tide of war seemed possibly to be turning in Britain's favour, all over the country our towns and cities began drawing up what were inevitably known as 'blueprints for the future'. In the October of that year, a group of delegates from the smaller towns met to consider their future in the brave new world that was going to be. Among them was a lady from CEMA (Council for the Encouragement of Music and the Arts) who sketched in the cultural requirements of a small town. One of her targets was the cinema. Only too often, she said,

the small town owed its contact with the world of ideas to the cinema alone ... The trouble is that the cinema is rarely a local institution: it is part of a commercial monopoly (and an international one at that), over-specialised, over-centralised and outside the scope of local interest and activity and outside local control.

But time here, as elsewhere, eventually turns truth into irony. In 1982, when the brave new world was well into its second generation, a group of citizens in Yarmouth, Norfolk, launched a campaign to save one of the last of its cinemas – the Regent – built by a local cinema magnate in 1914.

Throughout the thirty-odd years of its dominance, from the late 1920s until the advent of mass television in the late 1950s, the cinema was the object of sustained attack from middle-class intellectuals and moralists. It was eroding the 'Englishness' of England with a flood of Americana: it was undermining morals, creating discontent by holding up impossible goals of material satisfaction. Yet it is to be doubted if any other institution in the town brought more comfort to more people at a time when it was more desperately needed. The theatre was expensive and self-conscious – people went there as much to be seen as to see and it was almost exclusively middle-class. The churches were emptying, the pubs squalid. The cinema was one of the very few public places where an unaccompanied woman could escape from domestic pressure without being molested; children could use it; the poor could use it. For a tiny fraction of the family's small weekly income it was possible to get a view into a wider world in conditions of what appeared to be luxury. In *Angel Pavement*, published in 1930, J. B. Priestley painted a vivid – if disapproving – picture of the world into which a working-class lad could enter for a few pence:

They first walked through an enormous entrance hall, richly tricked out in chocolate and gold, illuminated by a huge central candelabra, a vast bunch of russet gold globes. Footmen in chocolate and gold waved them towards the two great marble balustrades, the wide staircase lit with more russet gold globes, the prodigiously thick and opulent chocolate carpets, into which their feet sank as if they were the feet of archdukes and duchesses. Up they went, passing a chocolate and gold platoon or two and a portrait gallery of film stars, whose eyelashes seemed to stand out from the walls like stout black wires, until they reached a door that led them to the dim summit of the balcony, which fell dizzily away in a scree of little heads.

Between 1932 and 1937 890 cinemas were built in England: by 1938 there were a total of 5000 of which 900 were owned by

Oscar Deutsch, a Birmingham scrap merchant who founded the Odeon chain in 1932. What is immediately striking about the cinemas of this epoch is their aristocratic names, deliberately evoking images of luxury. Every town now had its Carlton or its Embassy, its Majesty, Plaza, Ritz, or Capitol. Built at a cost of between £50,000 and £100,000 (at a time when a four-bedroomed detached house would cost under £1000) their interiors have been described as 'Babylonian Spanish-Cubist with chromium and bakelite trimmings'. Some twenty million people went to them once a week – at least 40 per cent of the population seeking their anodyne. Unlike the theatre, they had no bar (one of the puritan-isms invariably practised by the authorities when licensing working-class pleasures) but their tea-rooms, sharing something of the luxury of the rest of the building, became important social rendezvous.

They should have made an immense and permanent impact upon the townscape, these pleasure domes in whose construction no expense was spared. But the truly remarkable thing about them, perhaps, is how little effect they have had, their architecture proving as evanescent as the pleasures they purvey. Their façades, stripped of neon lights and billboards and splendidly uniformed commissionaires, sink back undetected into the urban scene. Those that survive as places of entertainment do so mostly as bingo halls – but the glamour has been rubbed from them like the dust from a butterfly's wing. One is reminded of Satan in Marie Corelli's turgid romance, himself a species of cinema magnate, speeding his guests with the diabolic equivalent of a neon-lit sign 'Sic Transit Gloria Mundi', before switching off the lights.

8

View in a Mirror

The most obvious gap in the records of the vast majority of English towns is the town chronicle. The absence of the chronicler is a characteristic of our history which contrasts unfavourably with that of almost any continental country and is one of the strongest indications of the rural idealism that informs English society. In France, Germany, the Low Countries and, above all, in Italy, most towns could point to a citizen – usually a merchant – who, inspired by no other reason than local patriotism, kept a form of diary recording the current activities of his town. The chronicles might vary immensely from bald entries made at irregular intervals to copious running narratives: their compilers might be barely able to write, or could possess a superb literary skill. Whatever their defects or pretensions they provided a framework of the history of their town denied to the majority of their English equivalents. The lack of the town chronicle is at once cause and symbol of the long English indifference to urban history: the official records might be present, but the enlivening mind of the contemporary commenting, questioning, judging, is absent. When, from the eighteenth century onwards, attention was directed towards local history, it was overwhelmingly weighted in favour of ecclesiastical architecture and the geneaology and property transfers of county families. A typical early nineteenth-century town 'history' would combine the two factors, painstakingly transcribing the epitaphs of the gentry in the parish church, while listing their possessions and endowments to the town.

But if we do not possess the chronicler, we do, from the earliest days of print, possess the traveller. And he, in due course, developed into that superbly English figure, the antiquary. Eccentrics though they may be, finding Druids under every stone and Romans under every arch, for all their frequent absurdities they lay the foundations of local history much as the alchemist, for all his absurdity, laid the foundations of modern chemistry.

The father of English topography was undoubtedly William of Worcester. He was born in Bristol in 1415, entered the service of Sir John Fastolf at Caister Castle in Norfolk, and retired to his home town when Sir John died in 1459. He made a major tour from Norfolk to Cornwall which formed the basis of his description, but it was in pottering round Bristol that he collected information which, though disregarded by those whose horizons were occupied by Romans and Druids, are of immense value today. His description and measurements of the streets and lanes of Bristol form one of the earliest factual descriptions of a town.

Worcester might be the first, but it is to the pages of John Leland's *Itinerary* that the enquirer turns again and again not only in quest for facts, but for the equally valuable subjective impressions (as with that picture of Bewdley glittering in the morning sun) which bring the facts of life. Leland was thirty years old when, in 1533, he received permission from Henry VIII to investigate the monastic libraries of the country and began the work which would occupy him for the remaining twenty years of his life. Ten years later, in a letter to the king, he claimed that

there is almost nother cape, nor bay, haven, creke or peere, river or confluence of rivers, breches, waschis, lakes, meres, forestes, fenny waters, montaynes, balleis, mores, hethes, woodes, cities, burgess, castells, principale manor placis, monasteries and colleges but I have seene them; and notid yn so doing a hole worlde of things very memorable.

It is in recording the break-up of the monastic system, which took place during his journeys, that Leland was particularly valuable. But he was fascinated by fortifications and by the different life-styles of towns. And with that lively eye of his he could pick on a characteristic, and sum up a place in a sentence. Droitwich is dismissed as a town famous for a single street – 'the towne itself is somewhat foule and dirty when any reyne falleth' – because the streets were badly paved. The buildings of Wakefield 'are meately faire, most of tymbre but sum of stone'; the strength of Newcastle's great walls 'far passith all the waules of the cities of England and most of the towne's of Europe'. And infusing all is that true, passionate love of country which motivated all these travellers and which Leland himself expressed in a letter to the king: 'I was totally enflammid with a love to see thoroughly all those partes of this your opulente and ample reaulme, that I had redde of.' Tragically, he went mad before he was able to order his notes into a coherent whole, and it was not until 1710 that they were eventually published.

Leland was essentially a field-worker. One receives the unforgettable impression of him jotting down notes while on horseback, intending later to flesh them out. William Camden was essentially an editor, willing to travel himself where necessary or possible but preferring to correlate the work of others, both living and dead, to create his great work *Britannia* (1586). Born in 1551, the year before Leland died, his was a purely academic career – Christ's Hospital, Oxford, then usher and headmaster at Westminster School and finally Clarenceux King of Arms. The title of his book is significant – England was, for him, the palimpsest that had been place upon Roman Britain: he even based its divisions upon the tribal organization at the time of the Claudian invasion. One gets little sense of the delight of discovery in Camden, but there are facts, neatly put together like so many Roman tiles; the name of the place, what it signifies, why it is where it is, who lives there, what it is worth.

With William Stukeley, we enter on to the first splendid flowering of the English antiquary. 'What Regions boast of more Antiquity and genuine Reliques of it of all sorts?' he asks rhetorically: 'What Earth throws up so many Roman Coyns, Medals, Urns &c that one would think Rome itself was transplanted in to Great Britain?' Born in 1687, Stukeley's career as a discoverer of England can be divided into two: the earlier, responsible period when, fascinated by Roman Britain, he set himself the task of tracking down its myriad manifestations and the later, undeniably eccentric, period when he was dominated by his Druidic obsession. The preposterous modern 'Druid' ceremonies at Stonehenge owe their origins to this amiable Anglican clergyman and his book *Stonehenge: a Temple restored to the British Druids*, published in 1740. But posterity owes him much for his careful – and exhausting – investigations into the Roman towns of Britain. On one of his tours, he walked along some 500 miles of Roman roads, describing not only the cities the roads connected, but the structure of the roads themselves. Of

Watling Street he remarked: 'It is laid very broad and deep with gravel not yet worn out, where it goes over commons and moors. It is raised a good height above the soil and so strait that upon an eminence you may see it ten or twelve miles before you.' He not only described and measured but also illustrated the great Newport Gate in Lincoln and the now disappeared Worth Gate at Canterbury, leaving a unique record.

Despite his enthusiasms and obsessions Stukeley, like Leland and Camden before him, was essentially a scholar. Celia Fiennes and Daniel Defoe who, between them though separately, covered most of the country between 1685 and 1725 were nothing of the sort. Celia Fiennes was a sharp-eyed, frequently sharp-tongued young woman who performed prodigies of travel on horseback simply because she liked travelling, and Defoe was a journalist in search of copy.

Celia Fiennes' remarkable journeys provide a considerable corrective to the popular picture of the roads of rural and provincial England as a savage and dangerous place before the nineteenth century. One wonders, indeed, whether a young woman today would penetrate into quite such remote areas with quite such insouciance. Born in 1662 into an aristocratic family near Salisbury, she began her journeys with her mother when she was twenty-three. Most of the journeys begin and end at the family manor house at Newton Toney or, later, in London. She claims that she was not writing for publication, but only for the entertainment of her close relatives. She and Defoe both displayed an indifference to – frequently a contempt for – the historic past. The only predecessor to whom she refers is Camden and his *Britannia*. But she manages to pack in a lot of background, as in her description of Salisbury – typically in her breathless, unpunctuated style:

From Newtontoney I went to Sarum 8 miles which is a Citty a Bishops Seate, pretty large town streetes broad but through the midst of them runs a little rivulet of water which makes the streetes not so clean or so easy to pass in, they have stepp's to cross it and many open places for horses and carriages to cross itt – it takes off much of the beauty of the streets – the cause of it was from the burning of the old town called Salesbury which was on a hill about a mile off this and it was so dry and farre from springs that it was destroyed by fire and only the ruines of the Castle is to be seen like a high wall with fortifications . . .

An incomplete version of the book was published, under the clumsy title of *Through England on a Side Saddle in the time of William and Mary*, in 1888, but it was not until 1947 that this sprightly view of England was published in its entirety. A new edition appeared in 1982.

Defoe began his tours in 1722, some twenty years after Celia Fiennes completed hers. Despite – or, perhaps, because of – his own failure at business, trade fascinated him: in every town he homed in on the market, questioning, poking around, nosing out facts about the principal trade of the town, as in those statistics he gives for Farnham corn market. But he is a journalist, too, deeply interested in the habits and customs of human beings, able to present them in a lively and sympathetic manner. His picture of the rather empty life of the fashionable taking the waters at Epsom is a delight.

You have no sooner taken Lodgings, and enter'd the Apartment, but if you are anything known, you walk out to see who and who's together; for 'tis the general Language of the Place – '*Come, Let's go see the town, Folks don't come to Epsom to stay within doors.*' The next Morning you are welcom'd with the Musick under your Chamber Window; but for a Shilling or Two you get rid of them, and prepare for going to the Wells.

In a page or so he takes the reader through a typical day, from the first gathering when 'you Drink the Waters or walk about as if you did: Dance with the Ladies tho' it be in your own gown and slippers' to the last ball or concert of the day.

Defoe is essentially urban in habits and interests: William Cobbett is his rural counterpart. Born in Farnham in 1762, Cobbett was a working farmer whose eloquence and pugnacity took him into politics. His 'Rural Rides' in the 1820s were undertaken for political purposes – to see and report on the condition of working people at a time of great economic and social change, but the observer triumphed over the propagandist. He can be violent, intemperate, prejudiced: his picture of a spa contrasts remarkably with Defoe's kindly account of the foibles of the fashionable. For Cobbett, Cheltenham – 'what they call a watering place' – was a sink of iniquity, a place to which East India plunderers, West India floggers, English tax gorgers, together with gluttons, drunkards and debauchees of all descriptions, female as well as male, resort at the suggestion of silently laughing quacks, in the hope of getting rid of the bodily consequences of their manifold sins.

He rejoiced at the apparent decay of the town – and incidentally gives some useful social facts:

The whole town (and it was now ten o'clock) looked delightfully dull. I did not see more than four or five carriages. The place really appears to be sinking very fast ... It is curious to see the names which the vermin owners have put upon the houses here. There is a new row of most gaudy and fantastical dwelling places, called 'Colombia Place' there is what a boy told us was the 'New Spa': there is 'Waterloo House' Oh how I rejoice at the ruin of the base creatures!

But when kindly disposed, he could leave an unforgettable portrait of the townsfolk going about their daily affairs: the farmers gathering for the 'ordinary' in the main inn of the town; children at play; families attending church.

Almost any novel by Dickens will yield gems of urban description. But the novel which best conveys the picture of provincial England busy on its small affairs is *The Pickwick Papers*. It has an inimitable atmosphere of freshness and gaiety, of a young man looking with eager eyes and immediate response to the world opening up around him. The device of creating a Corresponding Society, consisting of Mr Pickwick and his three 'young' followers who 'are requested, from time to time, to forward authenticated accounts of their journeys and investigations', allowed the young author to take his pen where he wished. The journeys of Mr Pickwick were confined to the south and east, from Bath to Bury St Edmunds via Kent and London. At Bath we meet the fashionable as they throng the Pump Room and Assembly Rooms under the mincing tutelage of Cyrus Bantam, MC. At Ipswich vigorous – and probably libellous – invective is hurled at the Great White Horse hotel, and has been gratefully used as publicity ever since: 'Never were such labyrinths of uncarpeted passages, such clusters of mouldy, ill-lighted rooms, such huge numbers of small dens for eating or sleeping in.' It is at the Great White Horse that Mr

Pickwick has his embarrassing encounter with the lady unwittingly sharing his bedroom – an encounter curiously counterparted in real life by William Cobbett. It is at Ipswich, too, that we meet the archetypal provincial magistrate, puffed up with conceit at his powers. But it is at Eatanswill that the country town is drawn three-dimensionally, affectionately, but also ruthlessly. We take part in the public breakfast given by the local poetess and lion-hunter, Mrs Leo Hunter. We witness the earth-shaking combat between the editors of the Eatanswill *Independent* and the Eatanswill *Gazette* and the hilarious corruption of the parliamentary 'election'. 'Everything was conducted on the most liberal and delightful scale. Excisable articles were remarkably cheap at the public houses; and spring vans paraded the streets for accommodation of voters who were seized with any temporary dizziness in the head.' *The Pickwick Papers* presents the picture of the English town just before it was overwhelmed by the result of the Industrial Revolution.

Through travel books like these, and through the monumental county histories that began to appear in the seventeenth century, it is possible to build up contemporary pictures of the town. But it is the town seen, in the main, from the outside by the traveller or the antiquary, bearing out the lament of the historian J. R. Green. Travelling in Italy in 1871 he wrote to a friend:

Roaming through these Ligurian towns makes me utter just the old groans you used to join in when we roamed through France, I mean over the state of our local histories in England. There isn't one of these wee places that glimmer in the night like fireflies in the depth of their bays that hasn't a full and generally admirable account of its doings and itself. They are sometimes wooden enough in point of style and the like, but they use their archives, and don't omit, as all our local histories seem to make a point of doing, the history of the town itself.

The mid-nineteenth century saw at least the beginning of civic self-awareness. Today, most public libraries will have massed on their shelves massive volumes, bound in dark green or brown, under some such title as 'Transactions' or 'Proceedings of the X Archaeological Society', Volume I of which will have been published about 1850. Looking at these unappetizing volumes it is difficult to realize that they contained the seeds of the extraordinary boom in archaeological publishing of recent years, the dusty lucubrations of long-forgotten scholars transformed into a glamour industry. But they contain, too, priceless monographs on the town, lovingly compiled by the new race of amateur historians. Local history has always been, and probably always will be, founded firmly on the work of the 'amateur' – to use the word in its correct sense of someone who performs a task of love, with no thought of financial reward.

The English town might not have its chronicler, but from the early eighteenth century onwards the chances are that it would have its newspaper and, as Lord Macaulay pointed out in one of his orotund periods, 'the only true history of a country is to be found in its newspapers.' These early papers, usually with some such title as 'Mercury' or 'Journal', were simply double pages which came out infrequently. But when Parliament withdrew stamp duty in 1855 almost overnight, it seems, scores came into existence. Guildford, which had a population of less than 5000 in the 1860s boasted no less than ten newspapers. Some lasted only a matter of weeks before their owners' editorial enthusiasm succumbed to commercial reality but others survived into the twentieth century, and continue to do so. One of the oldest running newspapers is the *Northampton Mercury*, launched in 1720 and still going strong, but most of the major towns of England can point to a similar long-lived publication.

The characteristics of the late nineteenth-century local newspaper were an immensely long title (usually obtained by a process of cannibalization), and addiction to crime, published in luscious detail, and a total indifference to libel. In his book *Exploring Cathedrals* Kenneth Hudson quotes a remarkable piece of invective that appeared editorially in the *Shropshire Conservative* in 1853, protesting against the establishment of Shrewsbury Catholic Cathedral.

As a nunnery is to be established to the Cathedral we shall, of course, have the town infested with Popish priests and these jesuits will prowl about seeking for victims. They will follow children into corners and byeways and with every blandishment possible endeavour to pervert the minds of their attendants. No man's house is secure from this espionage and no woman, married or single, safe from their lecherous designs. We do hope that these 'surpliced ruffians' will tenant their convent with saintly dames from Rousehill, the only fit companions for such a villainous set, who profess celibacy, and yet are constantly engaged in debauching the wives and daughters of their flock after degrading their minds in the filthy confessional.

The libel was gradually toned down, but even today the correspondence columns of the 'local rag' display an energy, and a degree of personal vituperation, long since departed from the nationals. It is in these columns, in the advertisements, and the news stories devoted to reports on local societies and events that the newspapers hold up a true mirror to their communities. Financially they may be overshadowed by the nationals (although significantly it is the local and not the national newspaper which leads with the introduction of new technology). But they continue to reflect what is a far more accurate picture of English life than do the London-based papers with their necessary formulae and simplifications. Lord Macaulay's dictum, if applied to the Eatanswill *Gazette*, still holds true.

Town guides began to appear towards the end of the century and their production has developed into a majority industry. Initially, their main objective was to attract new residents – well-heeled new residents – to buy the expensive new houses being built on the outskirts of the old towns. In the inter-war years, the emphasis changed to the desperate need to attract industry and, currently, the emphasis has shifted yet again, this time to tourism. The self-portraits presented by the guides is that presumed, in the main, to attract tourists, and their standard varies greatly.

The great historic cities, places like York and Winchester and Canterbury are served very well. So, too, are some of the smaller towns which are fortunate enough to have a good local printer working in conjunction with a good local historian or imaginative town council. The fact that at least half the press of a guidebook is devoted to advertising by no means reduces its value. It performs a real service to the visitor, who will be grateful to know where he can eat, sleep and have his shoes repaired, and it adds a considerable dimension to the social history of the town.

It is noticeable that the guides which really do reflect their communities are produced directly by the local authority. In most cases, however, the job has been contracted out to organizations specializing in something called 'municipal publicity' and the result is rather depressing. The text is usually anonymous, consisting for the most part of a relentless piling up of historical minutiae, couched in an unhappy mixture of estate agent's hyperbole and historian's jargon. Photography is dull, featuring only the most obvious of the town's set pieces and evidences of progress such as the bypass and the swimming pool. The modern town guide, in general, seems bent on perpetuating the English belief that municipal affairs must be dull to be respectable.

But there are, happily, straws in the wind. The series of so-called Mini-guides produced by the English Tourist Board, are excellent, with simplified plans, colour photographs and crisp authoritative texts that both whet the appetite for more and act as an adequate guide for a couple of hours. Even more valuable are the 'town trails' that have come into fashion over the past decade or so. In most cases they are the product of local history societies, subsidized perhaps by the local authority. The usual pattern is a simplified or isometric plan of the town centre, with the major buildings emphasized and the town's history developed out of a combined architectural and historic tour. It would be nice to think that some day all our towns, and not just a favoured few, will get a guidebook – a true mirror – worthy of them. Unless, the despondent thought occurs, they are doing so now.

In 1860 a certain Francis Frith loaded his pony and trap with one of the first 16″ x 10″ wet-plate cameras and set out to photograph the cities, towns and villages of England. In due course his sons took over the pilgrimage, building up a collection which has been authoritatively described as 'the most extensive important and well-preserved collection of early British documentary photography in existence'.

The Frith Collection is the most famous of all collections of local photographs. But the vast majority of towns in the latter part of the nineteenth century could point to some citizen who had become fascinated by the magical new technique, and lugging his massive wooden box camera round his native town recorded its life in the most poignant of all media. The railway stimulated tourism and this in turn stimulated the production of little guides – and endless postcards. As with so much of photography in its early, creative years, the standard is astonishingly high. But even more valuable from the point of view of posterity seeking a view back into the past, is the remarkable range of subjects covered. As opposed to the hackneyed half-dozen topics of today's postcards, they cover local industry, customs and everyday activities. As the town expanded, too, under the dynamism of Victorian confidence, the photographer was there to record yet another advance in the march of progress: the laying of the new sewerage system, the paving of the roads, the erection of the first gas-lights.

Fashions changed. The fragile glass negatives were destroyed in their thousands or put away and forgotten. Then, in that wave of nostalgia for the past which has been building up since the end of World War II, the survivors have achieved financial value and are being hunted out and reprinted. It is a profoundly moving experience to stand under the dim red light of a developing chamber and watch the past slowly forming itself again in a bowl of chemicals.

9

The Twentieth Century: Under Siege

In an invaluable check-list in his book *Local history in England*, W. G. Hoskins ranks in order of importänce forty-two provincial towns between the years 1334 and 1861, basing the earlier figures on tax potential and the later on population. Between 1334 and 1662 the same handful of towns jostle for the top six positions – Bristol, York, Norwich, Newcastle, Lincoln, Salisbury, Exeter, with occasional appearances from other historic cities. Using similar calculations, it would be possible to push the opening date back to the Conquest – in other words, for some 800 years the relative positions of the leading English towns remained largely unchanged. Then, in 1801, they all, except Bristol, vanish from the top six places and their places are taken by the new industrial giants – Manchester, Liverpool, Leeds, Sheffield, Birmingham. One could not find a more dramatic indication of the break or change in historic continuity.

Until the eighteenth century, the towns of England were each a species of island universe, separated rather than connected by an abominable road system that might have been created by savages. By the late seventeenth century, a few favoured places were connected by coach: in 1690 an advertisement appeared in Oxford boasting that 'A flying coach shall in one day perform the whole journey between London and Oxford during the summer half yeare (if God permit)'. But only the most strongly motivated travellers embarked on the journey from one town to another. As late as 1770 that sturdy traveller Arthur Young raised his voice to curse those responsible for the road that ran south from Newcastle: 'A more dreadful road cannot be imagined. Let me persuade all travellers to avoid this terrible country, which must either dislocate their bones or bury them in sand.' The creation of the Turnpike Trusts dramatically altered the pattern and frequency of traffic. Between 1760 and 1800 Parliament established over 1000 of these Trusts, each responsible for the upkeep of a section of road and entitled to raise tolls for their upkeep. Some quite small towns achieved unexpected importance because they were at the junction of a number of turnpike roads – five converged on the little town of Shaftesbury. And when, in the closing years of the eighteenth century, the road-making techniques pioneered by Telford and Macadam were adopted by the Trusts, England had the first fast, safe road system since that established by the Romans.

But it still operated over a limited area for those who could afford the high costs of travel. The probability is that a circle with a diameter measured in yards rather than miles would have encompassed the movements of the vast majority. Cobbett recounts a conversation he had with a villager who had never visited her local town four miles away. He asked her if she had ever been at Andover, six miles away.

'No' 'Nor at Marlborough?' (nine miles another way) 'No' 'Pray, were you born in this house?' 'Yes'. 'And how far have you been from this house?' 'Oh, I have been up to the parish and over the Chute.' That is to say, the utmost extent of her voyages had been about two and a half miles!

Cobbett, being Cobbett, did not fail to draw a moral in favour of the past from this story:

Let no one laugh at her, and above others let not me who am convinced that the facilities which now exist of moving human bodies from place to place are amongst the curse of the country, the destroyers of industry, of morals and, of course, happiness.

Cobbett died before the advent of the railway, the supreme facility for 'moving human bodies from place to place', an invention which would undoubtedly have given him apoplexy. And William Makepeace Thackeray, looking back over his own life from 1860, pinpointed the arrival of the railway as a moment of profound and universal change:

Your railway starts the new era, and we of a certain age belong to the new time and the old one. We elderly people lived in the pre-railroad world, which has passed into limbo and vanished under us. They have raised those railroad embankments up and shut off that old world which was behind them.

Thackeray's rhetoric gave colour but did not exaggerate. More than any of the inventions that were pouring out of the new-built factories, steam locomotion broke with the past for it was totally without precedent and the effect of its development could in no way be predicted. The Duke of Wellington was among those who thoroughly deplored the new invention, noting sourly that 'it would encourage the lower classes to move about' – an unusually perspicuous remark from His Grace. Innkeepers trooped forward to show how towns would die for want of trade as the railway swept potential customers onward at high speed. Canal trade would collapse, turnpikes come to an end. William Wordsworth wrung his hands:

> Is there no nook of English ground secure
> From rash assault . . .

But despite the opposition, the railway spread like some vast natural force. In 1843 there were some 2000 miles of track. Three years later, only an additional thirty-six miles had been built. But by the mid-1850s there were over 8000 miles and each year saw more towns brought into the network.

The pattern of life changed drastically under the impact of the Industrial Revolution. The towns, to start with, became infinitely more crowded. In 1790 there had been twice as many people living in the country than in the towns: in 1840, the position was almost exactly reversed. The already primitive sanitation systems were overwhelmed. In 1851 the Board of Health's inspector described a kind of horrific Cook's tour of the midden heaps of Haworth, referring to sites which can be identified today, such as the apothecary's shop where the midden was heaped up almost to the sill. 'In these middens are thrown all household refuse and offal from the slaughter houses where, mixed with night soil and with drainage from the pig sties, the whole lies exposed for months together, decomposition goes on and gives off offensive smells and putride odours.' He presents a macabre picture of the overcrowded graveyard: there were 1344 burials in ten years, the graves packed side by side under slabs which virtually paved the area.

Living in town centres became associated with squalor, disease and discomfort. The move to the suburbs began with a trickle of the wealthy, and became a flood of the less affluent as building societies came into existence. Government desperately tried to control the flood, passing planning acts which came too little and too late.

It is difficult to be objective about the suburbs. On the one hand, they have undoubtedly provided decent living conditions for millions of people. Twentieth-century man is, for all practical purposes, Suburban Man, for relatively few now live in the historic centres. But the suburb has diluted the town, shifting the centre of gravity from the heart of the place without providing an equivalent elsewhere. The advent of mass private transport has exacerbated the problem. Today, people in council and private estates are utterly dependent upon the car – the car, in fact, is the only solution to problems that the car creates. Those without access to private transport are dependent upon unpredictable, infrequent, expensive bus services for their social life. Few modern suburbs – the more expensive in particular – have any of the elements vital to town life: no church, no pub, no shop, no factory.

Meanwhile, the centres decay or are, increasingly, mummified. A photograph of almost any town centre in the 1930s shows a dreary picture of hoardings covering derelict buildings or empty houses, liberally pasted over with posters. They were distressingly vulnerable to the massive wave of post-war 'development', as the destruction of ancient buildings in order to maximize site values was termed. Frequently the bulldozer uncovered some gem of architecture that had been hidden by decades of accretion, such as happened in Hereford, when demolition of houses for an inner ring road in 1967 disclosed the city walls. This was a positive gain – but in that same year the old Ministry of Housing uttered the dire warning that: 'At the present rate we could rebuild every town in the country over again in fifty years – and the rate is still increasing. Large areas are taken for redevelopment, and a single new building may replace half a dozen old ones.'

Reaction against the rate of destruction, coupled with the growing obsession with the past, resulted in the current fashion of preservation. Sometimes the entire town is taken as a conservation project at a multi-disciplinary level with nothing but benefit for all concerned. Wirksworth in Derbyshire had hit the only too familiar spiral of unemployment, declining public transport, shrinking retail trade and a 'rapidly deteriorating stock of historic buildings'. In 1978 the Civic Trust launched Project Wirksworth, founded by an interlocking system of state aid and private charity. The ancient buildings were repaired with local labour, local skills; the Historic Buildings Council of the DoE launched a unified Town Scheme; COSIRA introduced four small factories and, inspired, the Abbey National Building Society departed from building society custom and offered mortgages for repair and renovation of old buildings.

But preservation can go too far, freezing and sterilizing a living fabric. Elm Hill in Norwich is a conservationist's *memento mori*. The city has a brilliant record in preservation, beginning back in the 1920s when most other cities were demolishing their 'worn out' old buildings in the interests of modernity. The city fathers decreed, in 1927, that Elm Hill, an ancient but decrepit street, should be preserved. It is possible to follow, through the letter columns of the local paper, the whole process from exciting beginning to embarrassing results half a century later.

First there is the city engineer's report in 1925, recommending total demolition of the ancient guildhall: 'There is little of interest here except a few beams and some wood mullion windows.' Two years later there is a hesitant reappraisal: 'Elm Hill is not in the true sense a slum.' Work starts on restoration, and is greeted with universal approval and delight. Elm Hill begins to feature prominently in tourist literature.

Then the residents of Elm Hill begin to worry a little. In 1951 there is a wistful request: 'I see the dog shop is now vacant. Would it not make a lovely fish and chip saloon.' The proposal is met with horror, but three years later the paper is editorializing: 'It is to be hoped that the street does not lose its character by becoming precious.' Over the next ten years, gentrification continues: small shopkeepers move out, antique shops and art galleries move in. But these, in their turn, are caught up in the apparently inexorable process. There is a proposal to ban traffic in the street and the traders are up in arms. 'If the council want to make a sort of museum of this street, they ought to pay us, instead of we having to pay them.' In 1974 there is a painful episode when an over-enthusiastic city council, now intent upon gilding the lily, substitute what critics called 'pantomime lamps' for the original sturdy street lamps, occasioning this comment from an ungrateful citizen: 'Here, in the heart of Norwich, in this insignificant byway, is the beginning of a project which is our own, our very own, contribution to European Disneyland Year.'

In town after town, traffic poses an apparently insuperable problem: does one allow it to choke the town, or ruin the countryside? The beautiful little town of Bakewell in Derbyshire was presented with this problem in an acute form. The town is badly congested during the summer months with tourist traffic – but the only possible alternative route would take the noisy, smelly, dangerous stream through meadowland between the road and the river. And as a contributor to *Country Life* noted:

If you stand on the river bank by the town bridge, where birds congregate and rainbow trout leap to snatch breadcrumbs almost out of picnickers' hands, or upstream at Holme where a packhorse bridge of 1694 spans the river, you see just why the townsfolk resist the suggestion whenever it comes up, as it does periodically since the 1930s.

And even when the decision is made, the nettle grasped and the traffic diverted, more problems are created.

In Wiltshire, a new trunk road – the A303 – came into being to take the intolerable pressure off the small towns along the A30, the old coach road to the south. It succeeded. But it also isolated them. Modern road engineering is marvellous for moving at speed but tends to forget that the purpose of travel is to arrive. The Department of the Environment, the current transport overlord, has its own esoteric rules about signposting: only for populations above a certain size, according to certain local conditions. Given the absence of signposting and the design of modern trunk roads, it is only too easy to speed past some ancient community and not even realize that it's there. At Salisbury, for instance, the round-abouts that surround the city whiz the traffic off southwards as though by centrifugal force so that one sees nothing of the city except for the cathedral spire. All this certainly protects the physical and environmental fabric of the town, but it has an appalling effect on the local trade on which the town ultimately relies. Accordingly, the towns along the old A30 – Salisbury, Wilton, Shaftesbury, Sherborne among them – in 1982 banded together to launch a tourist promotion scheme entitled 'Discover the A30' whose aim was to bring traffic back down the old coaching route.

Tourism is the great enigma of our day, the phenomenon that can bring lifeblood to a town, or destroy it in a manner that even the air raids of World War II, even the hungry depredation of developers could not achieve. On the one hand it is one of the few industries which thrives during periods of industrial depression. The raw materials are everywhere for the using, for every town has something to offer. The rise of industrial archaeology, for example, has directed attention – and much-needed cash – to the declining industrial towns of the north. Tourism is the only industry that can revive crafts and industries for which there is no longer economic justification. In Chester, a highly successful horse-drawn barge plies the canal carrying tourists.

But tourism can throttle and cheapen, as the Padstow resident noted. Cornwall is particularly badly affected. Each summer in Polperro on the south coast the unequivocal face of tourism is demonstrated. At peak periods, there are more visitors than there are residents, crammed into the single main street. 'It's wall-to-wall people,' a hotelier noted ruefully and, although he earns his living from them, he admitted: 'By the end of the summer you hate the sight of them, hate the sight of them peering through your windows.' From June onwards, the local authority operates a system reminiscent of the delightful comedy film *Passport to Pimlico*: only residents are allowed to take their own cars into the built-up area, all others being obliged to park outside. If there is no space – you just drive on down to the next town or village that can accommodate you.

Another phenomenon of the last quarter of our century is the rise of amenity or civic protection organizations. Town societies have been in existence since the late nineteenth century but as local authority has become ever more remote, with more and more powers going to a distant county hall, and as the demands of 'developers' grow ever more intolerable, so amenity organizations based on parishes, wards and even streets have sprung up. Like tourism, they are a two-edged weapon. On the one hand, they form an excellent channel for information, conveying to the citizens information about some developer's planned depredation in time to do something about it. The combined professional expertise of their members – lawyers, accountants, architects, journalists and the like all giving their services free – provides a formidable weapon. But they can also dissipate at parochial level energies badly needed at town level. At one expensive public enquiry, the contestants were two powerful amenity organizations, each seeking to have a bypass directed through the territory of its neighbour. Individuals have the same duality of motive, campaigning vigorously at one moment for the preservation of some favoured building, at the next lobbying as vigorously for the construction of a facility that will benefit them, regardless of its effect on the environment.

The town has been under siege for three decades now, mainly from traffic and from 'developers'. In 1961, the then President of the West Surrey Association of Building Trade Employers announced: 'Guildford must be regarded as a building site in process of being "redeveloped".' The arrogant assumption that a thousand-year-old town was in need of being 'developed', and that such 'development' could be done exclusively as an exercise in profit sounded the authentic note of the boom decades.

The enemy is still at the gates, vigorous as ever, but there are signs that the beleaguered garrison is learning to deploy its weapons effectively. The local authority has begun to resist the powerful road transport lobby, timidly at first but with increasing effectiveness with the creation of 'pedestrianized' zones in the town centre. Living in town centres is again becoming attractive partly through the soaring price of petrol. Terrace houses, so much more efficient in space utilization than the detached house, are again becoming fashionable. The return to the centres is, as yet, barely a discernible trickle, but it may well be the beginning of the tide.

Above all, the most effective recent measure has been the 'recycling' of ancient buildings that have lost their original purpose but still have decades – perhaps centuries – of life in them. In the 1920s and 1930s obedience to the fashion of 'modernity' dictated their destruction. From the 1960s onwards, the fashion of 'conservation' has begun to protect. Initially, such conservation was static, freezing the building at some ideal period and turning it into an 'ancient monument' for which there was no conceivable use. But increasingly, there is the recognition that such buildings can have economic use, a fact which not only restores them to life, but guarantees their future existence. King's Lynn – that little East Anglian town which has set a standard in townsmanship that many a giant would do well to copy – has transformed its old Hanseatic warehouse into council offices. Twenty years ago the buildings were virtually derelict. Their restoration in 1971, and subsequent use as offices, proved that aesthetics could have an economic justification. Swindon, in Wiltshire, provided an even clearer example than this when the Council acquired Brunel's old railway village for £118,000 – a cost price of around £300 for each house. Brunel had built this model village in 1841 to house the workers at the great locomotive works that were to be Swindon's major industry for the next century. The village decayed with the decline of the railways. In 1965 the inevitable 'developer' appeared with a proposal to demolish and build anew. There was a massive local reaction against the news and, in due course, the Borough bought the village. Conversion costs for each house worked out at about £2500. 'The current costs of building the same size unit today with modern construction techniques would be approximately £5,500,' the Borough Council announced with justifiable pride. The ratepayers of Swindon have been saved a substantial sum, several hundred citizens have acquired dignified homes and the town itself has received a handsome addition to its fabric. Aesthetics and economics can indeed go hand in hand, but for that one needs an imaginative local authority – not the commonest of creatures in the late twentieth century.

During the course of research for this book the author visited some sixty or seventy localities in England over a period of about two years. In almost every historic town – that is, in almost every town famed for the beauty and interest of its architecture and setting – at some point a resident was sure to remark: 'Ah, but you should have come here ten years ago [or fifteen years, or twenty years], before They built the supermarket [or demolished the Red Lion or constructed the new roundabout].'

It is as though, during the 1960s and 1970s, a vast tidal wave had roared across the country, sweeping aside town centres that had been centuries a-building, depositing immense new structures whose shapes were still alien to the eye. Here and there were exceptions. Ludlow is an outstanding example, where a combination of topography, sturdy local patriotism and plain good luck allowed the wave to be diverted. But elsewhere, the town that entered the 1980s was substantially different from the town that had entered the 1960s. It is highly instructive to compare an eighteenth-century town plan of almost any historic town with the town centre as shown on any Ordnance Survey plan before 1960. In almost every case, the eighteenth-century plan was quite a useful vade-mecum for the traveller before 1960. Today, any town plan more than ten years old is wholly misleading.

The tidal wave of 'development' was preceded by a blizzard of 'planning applications' – the legal requirements whereby a 'developer' was obliged to deposit with the local authority precise indications of his intentions. Such applications are, in fact, simply two-dimensional indications of impending three-dimensional changes which few laymen are capable of interpreting – and whose result, indeed, takes even the professional by surprise. In Guildford, the internal road system which had been constructed at vast cost and damage to the urban fabric in the 1970s was, in 1982, officially defined as 'a hostile environment' and *ad hoc* arrangements were made to protect, or divert, the citizen from it.

In town after town after town, therefore, those most affected by the advent of change were unaware of its implications until it had taken place. It was the speed and scale of this change, not the change itself, which disconcerted and alarmed the citizen, earning civic architecture its increasingly opprobrious reputation. The living town changes, as does any other organism. The Elizabethans substituted timber for stone; the Georgians clad timber with brick; the Victorians added curlicues to everything and began the invasion of the countryside. What was totally and horrendously unprecedented was the fact that a handful of men, with the aid of titanic machines, could, within hours, totally erase what had taken centuries to grow and could, within days, erect structures of a kind which had never been seen before in human history.

There have been four major agents of urban change: the population explosion, commercial 'development', road transport and electronic communication. Population explosion is unlikely to be reversed. There are signs that commercial 'development' is being arrested, but this is more likely to be due to economic recession than any permanent recognition of its furiously destructive qualities. In Britain, it has been commonly assumed that the destruction of the railway system – the ideal transport medium – is the work of a vast and sinister 'road lobby'. It may well be so – although it is significant that even in Soviet Russia, with its enormous spaces and less affluent population, this same system is in as bad a state as in the West. Man, it would seem, is a quadrirotal mammal. And, finally, electronic communication has reinforced the fragmentation triggered off by the motor car. The telephone makes it unnecessary to pop around the corner for a chat; television brings entertainment into the home.

In general, what we have done is to transfer the urban dynamic from public to private objectives, paradoxically creating miracles of domestic comfort, protection and entertainment within dreary, featureless urban environments. Looking at these four immensely powerful agents of change, and looking round at what they have wrought in the past three decades, the overwhelming temptation is to succumb to pessimism, to warn the next generation, in effect, 'Look your last on all things beautiful.' For one may reasonably suppose, on the basis of rational extrapolation from the present, that the town of the future will be a vast, sprawling, formless mass whose sterile centre holds a handful of fossilized 'protected buildings' and 'ancient monuments'.

But Man, happily, is not a wholly or even mainly rational animal and no profession is more hazardous than that of prophet – urban prophecy in particular. Again and again, over the centuries, the death of our towns has been pronounced. There is no need to go back to the abandonment of the Roman cities or to the era of the Black Death when our towns became tombs, or even to the mid-nineteenth century when they were threatening to choke on their own effluvia. In our own century we have seen basic changes of direction, when a seemingly irresistible slide towards destruction has been halted. Thus, *Country Life* reported of the town of Farnham in 1904: 'The town was at the nadir of history. But almost immediately the coming of the motor car began to raise the town from a decaying agricultural centre to one of increasingly prosperous business and residence.' No one in Farnham could possibly have predicted, in 1900, that the smelly, stuttering, comic horseless carriage was going to be a major agent of the town's salvation. No one could have predicted, in the 1890s, that the warning about our streets becoming impassable in the 1990s because of the piles of horse dung, would become a period piece.

Is there, one wonders, even now waiting in the wings some yet undreamed of concept that will provide the vital corrective at the vital moment? One can but hope.

Appendix

Descriptive notes on fifty English country towns, together with their probable place-name meanings.

Place-name science is full of traps. *Oxford* is, unsurprisingly, derived from 'ford for oxen' but *Oakham* has nothing whatsoever to do with oak trees. And who would have guessed that *Maldon* means 'hill with a monument or cross'? Nevertheless, a town's name carries within it a wealth of concentrated history – sometimes conveying a startlingly fresh viewpoint on its origins.

Many of the examples here are compacted. 'King's pool, for instance – the origin of *King's Lynn* – is understood to mean 'king's [manor of the] pool'.

Alnwick, Northumberland. 'Farm by the [river] Alne'. Pop: 7300. The ubiquity of the Percy lion (with its extraordinary tail sticking out like a poker) proclaims the feudal origins of the town, even while the name indicates its economic cause. Massive town gate still survives. The White Swan has done itself over, but unchanged is the remarkable *Olympic* suite, created out of the panelling of the lounge of the *Titanic*'s sister ship. Annual, recently revived 'mediaeval' fair.

Alresford, Hants. 'Ford over the Alder'. Pop: 3864. Planned town, laid out by Bishop of Winchester at about same time as Farnham (*qv*). Simple T-shape, with main road running along upper bar of T, but excellent example that *urbanitas* (significantly, no equivalent in English) does not depend upon size.

Alston, Cumbria. 'Aldhun's town'. Pop: 1916. Curiously, has the seedy charm of a Mediterranean town. Superb setting in rolling hills. Railway axed – but civilized bonus granted by turning track into footpath which takes one into the heart of the town. Market cross recently demolished by lorry.

Barnard Castle, Durham. 'Castle of Bernard [Balliol]'. Pop: 5430. Tucked away in this little town is one of the great museums of Britain – the Bowes Museum. The town merges into the vast, ruined castle, cannibalizing much of it. Dignified high-street-cum-market with outstanding market cross. Locals point with pride to the two tiny holes just visible in the weather-vane – bullet holes made by rival marksmen firing from Turk's Head, 100 yards away, in 1804. A robust society.

Bath, Avon. 'The [Roman] baths'. Pop: 79,965. Living example of the English ability to muck up a too-perfect plan and so make it liveable. The Woods' geometric town would have been just too much of a good thing, but a thousand subtle – and not so subtle – subsequent modifications have kept the shape but given it substance. View from the river is a stunning stage set, but the classical buildings around the Pump Room tug only a casual forelock to Palladio.

Bury St Edmunds, Suffolk. '[Saxon] fort of St Edmund's'. Pop: 24,000 (estimate). Another planned town laid out by an ecclesiastic – Abbot Baldwin in eleventh century – which still carries the imprint of its creator. Strong social polarity. The pubs (excellent index to a town's character) mostly either dreary working-class or warming-panned middle-class. Splendid inn – the great Angel, favoured by Dickens. Greene King Brewery continued tradition of brewing started by monks at the Abbey. Evidently active preservation society – historic buildings in superb condition.

Cambridge, Cambs. 'Bridge over [river] Granta'. Pop: 90,440. Town-gown dichotomy almost painfully evident. No relationship between mediaeval jewel at heart and uninspired nineteenth- and twentieth-century suburban development. This and its companion Oxford (*qv*) are about the only two towns in England which, in the continental manner, develop their own life-style independent of the capital.

Canterbury, Kent. 'Fort of the Kentish tribe'. Pop: 36,290. Best approached from the so-called Pilgrims' Way when the vast, graceful mass of Bell Harry tower suddenly appears. The new approach road, Rheims Way, a splendidly dignified piece of road engineering – though one has to penetrate lethal barrier of ring road to enter town. A tourist town that knows how to handle tourists with mutual dignity.

Chester, Cheshire. 'The fort'. Pop: 61,370. It must be 400 years and more since a ship sailed up to Chester's walls. The port which the Romans developed has long since been a racecourse and the water-tower where the shipmasters paid their dues now stands in a beautiful garden far from the sea. But the Mayor of Chester still carries the splendid title of Admiral of the Dee. The canal which came just too late to save Chester as a port is having a vigorous new life as a tourist amenity.

Chester, Sussex. 'Cissi's fort'. Pop: 20,940. The perfect walled city, a tiny working model of everything that should be found in a town, including a superb coaching inn. Probably claustrophobic in social atmosphere, for the Establishment of the enormous cathedral must dominate the little city. Ideal for the casual visitor.

Colchester, Essex. 'Fort on the Colne'. Pop: 79,600. Britain's first and oldest city. Although within commuter range of London (just 50 minutes by train) possesses strong provincial identity. Modern development has, if anything, more clearly defined the ancient town.

Cromer, Norfolk. 'Crows' mere'. Pop: 5720. Contradicts usual picture of East Anglia being flat by perching dramatically on a cliff. Narrow lanes, continental in feeling, the whole still carrying the ambience of a respectable Edwardian resort.

Dorchester, Dorset. 'Fort used for fisticuffs'. Pop: 13,880. The Bloody Assize (when 292 people were condemned to death) still a tourist attraction – Judge Jeffrey's lodgings and the gallows pointed out with some pride. The Tolpuddle Martyrs finished up here, too. Most of the Roman walls now gone, but the great amphitheatre known as Maumbury Rings (which long preceded Rome) still dominates the outskirts of the town.

Dorking, Surrey. 'Dwellers along the bright stream'. Pop: 22,410. Dramatically situated at a gap in the North Downs with the vast mass of Box Hill (National Trust) as a backdrop. Parish church has panache of cathedral. Splendid White Horse Inn. (Why didn't Phiz use this as model for his Marquis of Granby in *Pickwick Papers*?) Interesting central street pattern based on Y-shape. But a town, alas, intent on committing hara-kiri. Behind the High Street huge chunks have been carved out of the urban fabric for car parks.

Durham, Durham. 'Hilly island'. Pop: 29,490. Conveys, almost overwhelmingly, the crushing mediaeval power of bishop and baron: cathedral and castle between them occupy most of what is virtually an island high above the river. Private houses tucked in wherever there is space. The whole an extraordinary survival in an industrial area.

Ely, Cambs. 'Eel district'. Pop: 10,630. The name is a giveaway. Even though the 'Isle of Ely' has long since disappeared as a geographical entity, the town still rises out of the green and black sea of the fenland like a sudden island. Not too difficult to imagine Celia Fiennes' precarious ride over the flooded causeway to the town where she found 'frogges' even in her bedchamber.

Exeter, Devon. 'Roman fort on the River Exe'. Pop: 95,621. What the Luftwaffe spared, the 'developers' have done their best to destroy. City cut off from river by one of the most lethal traffic conduits ever conceived. But there are tough bones behind it all. Some good new buildings – Marks and Spencer's shop in the High Street reflects the massive pillared vernacular. Marvellous guildhall – with excellent little booklet describing it. Gaudy fronts on surviving historic buildings, echoing flamboyance of natives.

Farnham, Surrey. 'Fern estate'. Pop: 33,140. One of England's few successful planned towns, laid out by Bishop of Winchester. The ground plan bears strong resemblance to grid pattern of Roman *castrum* – probably coincidentally. Mainly Georgian, but ruins of magnificent mediaeval castle, once seat of Bishop. The beautiful sixteenth-century Bishop's Palace in superb condition.

Godalming, Surrey. 'Godhelm's people'. Pop: 18,840. Another 'gap' town, beautifully set among water-meadows. Currently, volume of traffic down the single main artery makes town life hideous and dangerous. Old-fashioned shops charmingly out of keeping with the supposedly 'trendy' image of Surrey. First town to be lit by gas.

Grantham, Lincs. 'Granta's estate'. Pop: 27,830. Despite the Midlands sprawl, and proliferation of new roads, you will get the feeling of penetrating northward, of following the Great North Road. Some good survivals at town centre: massive stone conduit, built in 1597 and used for watering horses up to World War I. Much weathered market cross. And the magnificent stone front of the Angel, where King John stayed, still very much a town pub.

Guildford, Surrey. 'Golden ford'. Pop: 58,470. Invariably type-cast by satirists seeking image for commuter gin-and-Jag belt. In fact, toughly independent community with strong sense of identity. Transient population of newcomers rests on core of deep-rooted natives. (The same names appear in the Tudor rent rolls and the current telephone directory.) Currently under heavy siege from traffic painstakingly introduced into town centre.

Haworth, N. Yorks. 'Enclosed homestead'. Pop: 3536. Curious to reflect, in this town of the high clean moors swept by great winds, that it had one of the highest death tolls through disease in the nineteenth century. Overwhelmed by tourists and workers in the Brontë industry, but still dourly Yorkshire. Steak à la Brontë in the pubs – but also pies and mushy peas. Thriving woollen mill.

Hereford, Hereford & Worcester. 'Army ford.' Pop: 47,652. Somewhat uninspired pedestrianized 'shopping precinct' has enormous advantage of protecting historic heart. Cathedral possesses two treasures which make a journey worth while – the remarkable chained library (did scholars really work in that dizzy, draughty, murky loft?) and the *Mappa Mundi*. Outstanding guide book (virtually a history) edited by the City Architect with contributions from various writers including Jan Morris.

Hexham, Northumberland. 'Warrior's estate'. Pop: 9820. Border town, and very much aware of the fact. The fourteenth-century Moot Hall resembles a fortified Italian *palazzo municipale* and for the same reason – protection from violence. Simple, elegant, effective covered market-place.

Ipswich, Suffolk. 'Gips farm'. Pop: 120,447. Planners' *memento mori*, a town murdered in the cause of office development. A few ancient buildings fossilized at town centre (Dickens' White Horse Hotel and the beautifully pargetted Ancient House) and one outstanding new development, the Willis Faber Dumas Building with its extraordinary reflecting walls. But, for the rest, dull anonymous office blocks intersected with racing streams of traffic.

King's Lynn, Norfolk. 'King's pool'. Pop: 29,990. Unhappily conceived programme of industrial expansion has buried this little gem of a town in a tacky setting. But once the formless outer sprawl is penetrated a perfect example of urban preservation is revealed.

Lincoln, Lincs. 'Lake'. Pop: 76,660. Nothing, but nothing in all England (or Europe for that matter) can equal the stupendous first sight of the cathedral from the south – stone trumpets soaring up from the high hill. Neither does closeness diminish excitement for the traveller is ascending all the time, looking upwards, until the heart of the place is reached. Important recent archaeological discoveries make more of the Roman town visible than has been seen for centuries.

Ludlow, Shropshire. 'Hill by the rapid'. Pop: 7466. The town to which any foreigner could be brought with pride. Architecture deservingly famous, but even more important is strong sense of civic pride and identity, finding expression in the Historical

Research Group, which publishes outstanding papers on local history. Lots of little shops – particularly the superb pie shops which fuel the North. Ludlow Festival, based on castle, immensely popular, bringing in thousands of visitors. A few ominous hints of change – antique shops and second homes – but still a town run by and for its citizens.

Lyme Regis, Dorset. 'King's stream'. Pop: 3460. Small seaside town that somehow retains identity even when submerged by candy-floss-eating hordes. Nineteenth-century shops in high street: traditional tea shops still flourishing. The Cobb, elegantly curving breakwater which generated much of local fishing industry, considerable distance from town. Powerful current symbiosis of town, book (*The French Lieutenant's Woman*) and film – 'Visit the town to see the background of the film of the book'.

Maldon, Essex. 'Hill with a cross'. Pop: 14,350. Ironically, the axing of the railway probably saved this beautiful little town on its high hill, for it is well within commuting range of London. The great sailing barges on the river are now prestige or holiday craft – but are at least still working. The 200-year-old salt industry is also flourishing, and there is a strong revival in its equally ancient companion – oyster farming.

Norwich, Norfolk. 'North town'. Pop: 122,270. Although its size, strictly, takes it out of the 'country town' league no discussion of English architecture could omit this queen of cities. Survived the 'development' onslaught of the '60s and '70s with some gains. One of the first towns to enunciate proposition 'Where the car need not go, the car shall not go' and pedestrianize much of historic centre. Cattle market banished to outskirts but general market (everything from cockles to boots and shoes) goes its rip-roaring way under shadow of city hall. One blot: the endlessly sprawling genteel suburbs gulping farmland at alarming rate.

Oakham, Leicestershire. 'Occa's estate'. Pop: 6780. Heart of the Rutland freedom movement. They lost, alas, but Oakham is still a little country capital. Castle with bizarre horseshoe 'tolls'. (Distinguished visitors are still charged a levy of a horseshoe to mark their visit, Prince Charles being the most recent.) Market cross with stocks.

Oundle, Northants. 'The undivided people'. Pop: 3470. The School not so much dominates the town as permeates it. During term time, the whole place swarms as schoolboys hasten from one teaching block to another. Curiously, although there is a massive history of the school and historians have been quartered there for generations, there is neither history nor even a guide book of the town. Worth visiting for the Talbot (one of England's many 'oldest inns') alone.

Oxford, Oxon. 'Ford for oxen'. Pop: 98,521. England's answer to Florence. Despite the vast industrial presence of Cowley, and the overwhelming beauty of the historic centre, there is no sharp physical distinction between 'town and gown' as in its companion, Cambridge. The one really does seem to flow into, and be related to, the other.

Penzance, Cornwall. 'Sacred headland'. Pop: 19,360. If you leave St Ives early in the morning you can walk across England in a day and reach this pleasant, unassuming little town by tea-time. Palm trees contrasting with harsh coast of north Cornwall. Nearby, the astonishing St Michael's Mount (National Trust), rearing out of the sea like something from an Arthurian legend.

Richmond, Greater London. 'Rich hill'. Pop: 157,867. Included here as a curiosity. Despite vast swollen population, and fact that it is within clutch of London, somehow maintains central identity. At a nodal point of a quite terrifying traffic system – it is possible to stand on a road bridge and be simultaneously aware of noise produced by road, rail, water and air transport. But the famous view of the Thames from the top of Richmond Hill still survives, and so does Richmond Park to give some shape to town.

Richmond, N. Yorks. 'Rich hill'. Pop: 7440. The castle towering above the river and dominating the bridge is the ultimate romantic ruin. Relatively huge, uncluttered market place. Handsome cobbles everywhere and exquisite Georgian theatre. Ugly suburban sprawl on hills but citizens make good use of their beautiful, tumbling river.

Ripon, N. Yorks. '[Place of the] Hyrpe tribe'. Pop: 12,580. Though Pevsner rates the cathedral as among the ten most interesting buildings of England, it is disappointing to a layman – heavily restored, with everything immediately evident. No disrespect to Ripon to say that much of its charm lies in fact that it is an easy town to get out of – down the steps past the cathedral and the river and fields are immediately gained. Some delightful architectural survivals, including the Wakeman's house. And, pre-eminently the eerie continuity of the horn-blower – 800 years or more of unbroken tradition.

St Albans, Herts. '[Abbey of] St Albans'. Pop: 50,293 (1965 figure). Unlike its Roman peers, quite clearly conveys the impression of two separate townships, Roman and mediaeval with a third (nineteenth/twentieth century) town added to the mediaeval. Lots of space at town centre, green around the great Abbey, metalled in the handsome though cluttered market place. Another of 'England's oldest inns' here – the Old Fighting Cocks.

St Ives, Cornwall. '[Church of] St Ivo'. Pop: 9760. On the face of it, the seaside town that has everything: lapped by improbably turquoise sea, furnished with genuine fishermen, genuine coast-guards, genuine winding alleys and a museum of the works of one of the great sculptors of our time, Barbara Hepworth. But the whole seems a stage set, probably because of the infestation of 'craft shops', 'studios' and the rest. Overwhelmed by tourists in summer, comes into its own in winter.

Salisbury, Wilts. '[Saxon] fort at Soruiodunum'. Pop: 35,460. Busy provincial capital, amiable to tourists but getting on with own affairs. Fascinating buildings well maintained. The ring road acts as a kind of moat. Newly-elected MP, they say, still obliged to sing Wiltshire Song from balcony of great Hart Inn.

Shaftesbury, Dorset. '[Saxon] fort of Sceaft'. Pop: 4000 (estimate). Gold Hill has received ultimate accolade of being setting for TV ad. (The advertiser generously contributed £10,000 for repair to cobbles – giving an idea of what it costs to keep our ancient towns in good repair.) The Royal Chase Hotel used to be a monastery. Tiny museum (repository of the mysterious Byzant) lovingly maintained by voluntary workers.

Skipton, N. Yorks. 'Sheep farm'. Pop: 12,560. Public library – a splendid Victorian survival – evolved from Mechanics' Institute. Castle modestly tucked away, though entrance almost on high street. Fascinating complex of stream and canal running immediately below castle and behind, though within easy reach of the town. Public-spirited citizens are restoring the magnificent mill. Handsome high-street-cum-market made murderous by traffic.

Stamford, Lincs. 'Stony ford'. Pop: 12,000 (estimate). A town that demands superlatives: the despair of photographers for every building seems to be photogenic. Marvellous rambling George inn with arrogant 'gallows' sign; dignified almshouses; Queen Elizabeth's Treasurer William Cecil, Lord Burghley stretched out in marble in the parish church. But above all, it is the homogeneity of stone that stays in the memory.

Wareham, Dorset. 'Estate by a weir'. Pop: 4630. Tiny town with influence transcending its size for all roads go to Wareham (on the Isle of Purbeck, at least). River a living part of town – sea-going yachts come up majestically through water-meadows to tie up by town bridge. Court Leet still meets – though now only as a quaint custom.

Wells, Somerset. 'Springs'. Pop: 8960. Although population has soared recently, still one of our delightful anomalies – a city with a population less than many a village. The 1947 Planning Act came just in time to protect the two superb entrances from Bristol and

Shepton Mallet, where the country comes right up to the historic town.

Winchester, Hants. 'Fort called Venta'. Pop: 31,620. England's ancient capital still retains its dignity. Like Ripon its enormous cathedral is astonishingly reticent: one is unaware of its presence a few feet away from the High Street. Small museum in surviving gate house. Brilliant restoration and 'recycling' of the old Abbey of Hyde (Alfred the Great was buried here – but his bones were casually thrown away in nineteenth century). The precincts are now an imaginative residential area.

Worcester, Hereford & Worcester. 'Fort of the tribe of Wigoran'. Pop: 74,790. They still make *the* sauce here – you can smell it as you come in on the train. Still the best place to find Worcester porcelain. Crazy traffic system with cathedral cut off by hurtling stream, and buses forced to mount pavements. King John rests in the majestic cathedral – which also has magnificent library.

Wymondham, Norfolk. 'Estate of Wigmund's people'. Pop: 9390. Vast residential area tacked like goitre on to the historic town, but visitor need not be aware of it. Market cross like something by Arthur Rackham: splendid inn splendidly named – Green Dragon. But over all are the vast twin towers of the ruined abbey. Poignant little war memorial: 138 dead in World War I, 41 in World War II. Every family in the tiny town must have known war-engendered mourning.

York, N. Yorks. 'Eburo's place'. Pop: 99,787. The doyen of all English towns, whether viewed in terms of its history, its architecture or its current preservation. Rome infuses it – but so do all other periods. One of Europe's most imaginative museums recreates the entire ambience of past periods. River is a major feature. Memory of Richard III honoured everywhere. Favourite game: dominoes – the pieces clutched in one vast hand. Was the Yorkshire hand bred for Yorkshire dominoes – or vice versa?

Bibliography

Aston, Michael & Bond, James *The Landscape of Towns* (Dent, 1976)

Beresford, Maurice *New Towns of the Middle Ages*, 1967

Biddle, Martin 'Excavations at Winchester' in *Antiquaries Journal*, Nos 47, 48, 50, 52 (1968–72)

Binney, Marcus & Burman, Peter *Change and Decay: the Future of our Churches* (Studio Vista, 1977)

Burgess, Pamela *Churchyards* (Society for Promoting Christian Knowledge, 1980)

Butler, Lionel & Given-Wilson, Chris *Medieval Monasteries of Great Britain* (Michael Joseph, 1979)

Camden, William *Britannia* ed. (from the 1789 edn) Gordon J. Copley (Hutchinson, 1977)

Chamberlin, E. R. *Guildford* (Phillimore, 2nd edn 1982)

Cobbett, William *Rural Rides* abridged and edited by E. R. Chamberlin (Constable, 1982)

Council for British Archaeology *The erosion of history: archaeology and planning in towns* (1972)

Country Towns in the Future of England: a report of the Conference (Faber, 1944)

Cox, J. Charles & Bradley Ford, Charles *The Parish Churches of England* (Batsford, 1935)

Defoe, Daniel *A Tour Through England and Wales* ed. G. D. H. Cole (Peter Davies, 1928)

Dickens, Charles *The Posthumous Papers of the Pickwick Club* (Chapman & Hall, 1913)

Diocese of East Anglia *Thirteen-hundredth Anniversary Official Handbook* (1930)

Dyos, H. J. (ed.) *The Study of Urban History* (1968)

Gregory, Roy *The Price of Amenity* (Macmillan, 1971)

Gross, Charles *The Gild Merchant* (Macmillan, 1890)

Hoskins, W. G. *Local history in England* (Longman, 2nd edition, 1972)

Hoskins, W. G. *The Making of the English Landscape* (Hodder, 9th edition 1970)

Hudson, Kenneth *Exploring Cathedrals* (Hodder, 1978)

Hudson, William & Cottingham Tingey, John *The Records of the City of Norwich* (Jarrold, 1906)

Johnson, Paul *The National Trust Book of English Castles* (Weidenfeld & Nicolson, 1978)

Jusserand, J. J. *English Wayfaring Life in the Middle Ages* (Fisher Unwin, 1891)

Lang, Lloyd & Lang, Jennifer, *A Guide to the Dark Age Remains in Britain* (Constable, 1979)

Leland, John *The Itinerary 1535–1543*, ed. Lucy Toulmin Smith (Leland, 1907–10)

Ludlow Research Paper No. 2 *The Corner Shop* by David Lloyd and Madge Moran (1978)

Ludlow Research Paper No. 3 *Broad Street: its houses and residents through eight centuries* by David Lloyd, with illustrations by Stanley Woolston (1979)

Morris, Christopher (ed.) *The Illustrated Journeys of Celia Fiennes* (Webb & Bower, Macdonald, 1982)

Morris, Richard *Cathedrals and Abbeys of England and Wales* (Dent, 1979)

Morseley, Clifford *News from the English Countryside 1750–1850* (Harrap, 1979)

Norwich Corporation *Report of the City Committee as to the City Wall* (1910)

Parker, Rowland & Oswald, Arthur *Men of Dunwich* (Collins, 1978)

Platt, Colin *The English Medieval Town* (Granada, 1979)

Priestley, J. B. *English Journey* (Heinemann, 1934)

Richards, J. M. *The National Trust Book of English Architecture* (Weidenfeld & Nicolson, 1981)

Savage, Sir William *The Making of our Towns* (Eyre & Spottiswoode, 1952)

Stukeley, William *Itinerarium Curiosum* . . . (1724)

Sykes, Homer *Once a Year: some traditional British customs* (Gordon Fraser, 1977)

Townsend, James *News of a Country Town* (OUP, 1914)
Wilson, Roger, J. A. *A Guide to the Roman Remains in Britain* (Constable, 1975)

Acknowledgements

The author and publishers would like to thank J. B. Priestley and Messrs Heinemann for their permission to quote from *Angel Pavement*. The translation of the Anglo-Saxon poem 'The Ruin' is from Professor Gordon's volume of Anglo-Saxon poetry, in the Everyman series, by permission of J. M. Dent & Sons Limited.

PICTURE CREDITS
The author and publishers would like to thank the following for supplying black and white photographs for the illustrated section:

J. & C. Bord 1, 2 above and below, 4; National Trust 5 above, 6.

The illustrations on pages 3 above and below, 5 below, 7 and 8 were supplied by the author.

Index

Page numbers in italic type refer to illustrations.